PROFIT VS. PROSPERITY

OUTDATED ECONOMICS UNDERMINES THE COMMON GOOD

RICHARD H. MCGUIRE

BLOOMINGTON, MINNESOTA

ISBN 978-1-7365162-0-1 (soft cover)
ISBN 978-1-7365162-1-8 (ebook)

Library of Congress Control Number: 2021900997

All images in the book are created by the author
or used by permission of sources cited.

Cover and interior by Mayfly Design
Editor Marly Cornell

10541 Oregon Circle
Bloomington, MN 55438
rmcguire@eknrail.com

CONTENTS

INTRODUCTION

A NEW LOOK AT A COMPLEX ECONOMIC SYSTEM

Far too often, inquiry in the field of economics, on the micro and macro level, begins by asking the wrong questions—implicit questions such as: how does this part of the economy work? Why does it work this particular way? How will a change in one part of the system affect other parts of the system? The study of economics should not start with "How does it work," but rather, "How *should* it work?"

The "market" is an economic system that is understood and viewed differently depending on the context. Bring it up in many discussions, and passions can run high—pro and con. To some, "the market" is the altar of civilization. Hardly a dilemma cannot be resolved most wisely by the market. The market can allocate anything, adjudicate any commercial dispute, solve any problem society faces—indeed it has moved American society forward on many fronts for 200+ years. Some will argue that Americans are better fed; have access to more education, drink cleaner water, breathe cleaner air, spend less time on subsistence chores, live longer, and on and on. Some think the market can solve everything that ails us, much like a magic elixir sold from the back of a wagon in the early twentieth century. But to others, the market is a source of evil that afflicts just about everything that ails society economically and socially. As with most disputes, the truth likely lies somewhere in between.

While the market can certainly do some things well, it cannot handle all commercial situations, and it is not at all equipped to deal with some. This book provides an analysis of some of the ways in which the market has not delivered what many have come to expect, and shines a light on where the market has failed to deliver acceptable outcomes in a number of areas.

The shortcomings of the market can be addressed from a number of different perspectives as with any intellectual endeavor or effort. To determine the truth about something, they key driver is to ask the right questions that will hopefully lead to the right answers. Herein I pose some questions and suggest answers that will hopefully lead to valid conclusions. I will also discuss the reasons for market failures and offer some prescriptive ideas about what changes are needed.

The word market is subject to a variety of definitions and understandings as it is used so often and freely in daily discourse. Asking a room full of people to define what they mean by the market will likely produce a room full of answers. Outside of the field of economics, and at times within the rigor of economics itself, the term is much akin to the Indian fable about the blind men and the elephant. The elephant (in this case being the market) is defined by the beholder (the blind men) in terms of what part of the market an individual is in touch with. Yet no matter what we think the market is, most people in the developed world, and an increasing block of the developing world, view the market as a necessary ingredient to their individual success and well-being as well as the prosperity of their country as a whole.

When speaking of the market, the notion in most people's minds is actually a broader concept that combines the capitalistic system with components of the market—capitalism being defined as "an economic system characterized by private or corporate ownership of capital goods, by investments that are determined by private decision, and by prices, production, and the distribution of goods that are determined mainly by competition in a free market." (*Merriam Webster*)

Discussion of the market in this book refers to the US capitalistic free market system—what I suspect most people envision when they use the short-hand term "the market." General vernacular is followed, market referring to the overall economic system.

So what is this market, this capitalistic economic system so many talk about with so little precision? The many pieces and moving parts make up the multitude of written laws and regulations and societal norms and values that have evolved over more than 250 years in the US—the structures developed to price and trade labor and commodities. The fundamental role that the law plays in the US economic system at the federal, state, and local levels plays is readily apparent.

Interconnected components to this complex market system are legal, social, political, and economic. Economists invest a great deal of time studying the US economic system, trying to understand how the system works and how the various parts of it interact with each other. Economics tries to answer questions such as: what happens to B if we change A. Examples: If interest rates rise by 2 percent, what is the effect on the housing market? How do individuals react to changes in gas prices, or drops in the stock market? If changes are made to the tax code, what will the effect be on the incentive to work or save or spend? Do people lose the incentive to work when social safety nets are made too strong? What factors do people take into account when making personal financial decisions, and when they are evaluating risk?

The areas of inquiry are endless, and they are most certainly valuable. We cannot possibly know how the system works, or how changes to parts of the system may affect the whole, without serious inquiry into these types of questions.

Economists play a significant role in guiding the direction society moves over time. Consider the significant existential difference between the work of economists and social scientists and the work of biologists, chemists, physicists, and other practitioners of the hard sciences. The latter disciplines delve into and study systems and laws inherent in nature. Those laws of biology, chemistry, and physics have been with us for billions of years. DNA carries the blueprint of life. Two oxygen atoms will link with a carbon atom to form CO2. The laws of gravity exist on earth and throughout the universe. Scientists continue to delve deeper into these areas and learn more and more about the rules that govern these sciences, and the knowledge base of these disciplines has advanced dramatically over the last three centuries. Biology has moved from deciphering evolution to growing body organs in a laboratory.

Physicists study a cosmos that began billions of years ago and will end billions of years from now regardless of any human input. Chemists, biologists, and physicists study what many people say God created. But economists are studying what man has created—a system that is 100 percent man-made. The economic system and virtually every component of it could be changed tomorrow if we chose to make it so. I do not suggest that this is a shortcoming for economics, rather it empowers economics in ways that hard sciences do not. Economists can go in two different directions: they can study the existing system and ask non-trivial questions about cause-and-effect and outcomes (descriptive analysis), or they can ask even more profound questions about outcomes the system is delivering and suggest necessary and appropriate changes to that system (prescriptive analysis). The former line of inquiry is significant; the latter can change the course of history.

A current trend in thinking in the US (and spreading globally) is that the capitalistic market-based system as it exists in the United States is the optimal way to order the economic lives of Americans. And it may be. We can look back a few short years to the communistic system of organizing an economy (an experiment undertaken in Russia, its satellite countries, and others such as China), which seems to have failed. We can look east to the state-directed economy of China and countries in its sphere of influence, and we can see a clear leaning in the direction of the economic order in the US.

However, the danger in this movement around the globe is an inherent sense that it is all part of an organic, evolutionary process that is inexorably leading to the same economic system that is essentially in place in the United States. Remember: the current economic system is 100 percent man-made. It is not organic; it did not evolve. We built it. If it serves us well, we should be pleased with what we have constructed; whenever it does not serve us well, we need to change it.

A constant progression of change in the way people organized their economic relationships has existed from the earliest times when people first organized themselves into functioning societies. Tribal systems developed early on and were found around the globe, in the Middle East, in medieval European countries, in the developing parts of Africa, and Central and South America. Tribal systems within which civilizations were structured also dictated the economic relationships among people. In most tribal systems, leaders owned most of the resources and collected payment in one form or another from the rest of the common people, often a percentage of the crops grown.

Tribal systems gave way in Europe to a feudal system during mediaeval times, which controlled how villages and regions were organized for farming, land use, and defense against other neighboring regions. They also dictated the rules under which commerce and the economy functioned. Serfs paid rent to their "land" lords who in turn provided them with land to farm and protection from invaders. This system eventually gave way to mercantilism in Europe during the period roughly between 1500 and 1800.

Mercantilism built strong walls around the economy of each

sovereign state and functioned on several economic theories long since discarded, e.g. trade between countries is a zero-sum game in which every country attempted to run a trade surplus. (LaHaye, "Mercantilism.") Then along came the industrial revolution, Adam Smith, and a multitude of economists and political economic theorists. Two hundred years later, here we are.

A brief look at the components of the current US economics system illustrates what I mean when I say the system was created by the mind of man. If you dig deep enough (and it does not require a great deal of excavation), it is clear to see why each piece of the system is the way it is. To put it simply, we have created an economic system that has three key components, legs if you will: legal, social, and political, which can be described and understood in the following ways.

Legal: The skeleton of the US economic system is the vast swath of laws that dictate how it works. A significant part of the body of law in the US sets out how economic relationships are to function between the state and corporations and individuals, between corporations, between corporations and individuals, and between individuals. These laws cover topics as far-reaching as the formation of contracts, enforcement of contracts, taxation, creation of property rights, enforcement of property rights, rules for understanding and interpreting business practices, licensing requirements of lawyers, doctors, and teachers, and on and on. Over the past 250 years in the US, Americans have developed a system of laws dealing with the ownership and transfer of property; taxation of income, consumption, and wealth; creation and enforcement of contracts; resolution of commercial disputes; and more. New laws have been written and old laws repealed to accommodate changes in commercial relationships between one another as technology has changed, values have changed, and attitudes have changed.

The corporate legal structure in the United States was slowly formulated during the late eighteenth century and early nineteenth century, and the rights accorded corporations have expanded ever since (Arner, 2002). Prior to that time, business was conducted primarily either under the form of a sole proprietorship or a partnership. Individuals realized they had much less risk managing their business if they separated their business life from their personal life and their personal assets. This led to the creation of the corporation as we know it and the doctrine of limited liability. Over time, corporations acquired powers and attributes that used to be reserved for individuals. Consider Citizens United v. Federal Election Commission, 558 U.S. 310 (2010), which granted corporations the right of free speech. Changes in the law of corporations have been steady and profound since its inception. In the 1860s, slaves were not people; but by 2012, corporations were considered the same as people with many of the rights held by individuals.

Almost any law or regulation dealing with commerce was first written at some point in time at the instigation of an interested party who, as they say, "had a dog in the fight." For example, Congress passed the Sherman Antitrust Act, 15 U.S.C. §§ 1-38 in 1890 to rein in the growing monopolistic power of companies that were combining under the form of trusts controlled by the same individual. One of the trusts sought to be prevented from monopolistic tactics was the Standard Oil Trust created in 1882 by John D. Rockefeller.

In 2005 Congress made sweeping changes to the bankruptcy laws with the passage of the Bankruptcy Abuse Prevention and Consumer Protection Act of 2005, Pub. L. No. 109-8, 119. Stat. 23. The requirements for filing for total liquidation of debts under Chapter 7 of the law were made more stringent, along with many other changes, requiring means testing to determine if an individual could file for protection under Chapter 7 (total liquidation of debts) or Chapter 13 (reorganization of debt). The changes were initiated by bankers and others in sectors of the financial industry who convinced lawmakers that debtors were taking advantage of them, escaping too easily from their duly contracted debts. These examples illustrate how laws dealing with commerce that lay down "rules of the road" for the economic system are constantly being changed and then reworked again in response to some interested party's request.

Social Structures: Arguably one of the most deeply imbedded and significant social structures affecting the economic history of the US was slavery. Slavery was the economic engine that powered the southern states all through the eighteenth century and midway through the nineteenth century. The southern agricultural economy was built on the institution of slavery and the plantation system. Without the cheap labor that slavery provided to the South, the ensuing history of King Cotton and the tobacco industry would have been quite different.

Beginning at the Philadelphia Convention in 1787, the framers of the US government, by most accounts intelligent and well-intentioned men, argued over how to count slaves as people for purposes of tallying the population state by state for taxation and representation purposes. States paid taxes to the federal government based upon the number of citizens in each state, and states were allocated seats in Congress based upon the number of citizens in each state. The compromise finally reached between northern and southern states was that a slave counted as three-fifths of a person.

Slavery had begun in the US in 1690 when the first slave ship arrived in Virginia, and it was in some people's economic interest to have free labor. Slavery powered the South's economy for over 150 years, almost destroying the country in its final years. It was finally abolished in 1865 with the stroke of a pen and a terrible bloody civil war leading up to that moment. A majority of the people could no longer tolerate the injustice and inhumanity of slavery, and one person, Abraham Lincoln, signed the Emancipation Proclamation, a presidential proclamation and executive order.

Slavery was created by men and was ended by men. No natural evolutionary process existed whereby the US economic system, for some period of time, had to have this form of free labor, and then 150 years later presumably evolved to a place where it was no longer needed. A few men, including several of the Founding Fathers, benefited from it, so it developed. Many people were repulsed by it, so it ended.

Similarly, the full inclusion of women into society, which has huge economic implications for a nation, was slow to take hold in the US. The passage of the 19th Amendment in 1920 finally granted women the right to vote in federal elections.

The failure to educate women in any country (women generally make up about 50 percent of the population in most countries) has been shown to have a crippling impact on a country's economic development. Failure to allow women to participate in the political process, the process which in many ways sets the ground rules for the economic system, clearly mutes their input in writing the rules of the game. Changes such as women's suffrage did not come easily or quickly. Thousands of people argued, demonstrated, and died before this change took place. Such things are amenable to change at the will of the people.

Political: Political debate is a complicated mix of peoples' personal philosophies, biases, and prejudices, mixed in with their life experiences and knowledge base. Political perspectives are ever-changing. Nonetheless, they have a terribly significant impact on the economy, the market, and how it changes. Politics ask important questions that directly impact US markets. How much power should the states have, and how much should the federal government have? What rights do people have as citizens of the United States? What are those true intrinsic rights? How far can labor go in organizing collectively? Who can meddle in the development of grade school and high school curricula? What qualifications does a person need to be licensed to practice a particular trade or profession (electricians, hair stylists, doctors, attorneys, teachers)? Should sales taxes be levied on transactions conducted on the internet? The questions asked in the political arena are seemingly endless and incredibly diverse. Yet the answers to so many of them directly affect the structure of the market.

One "political" question emphasizes this point vividly. If there has ever been a political hot button issue in the US, it is immigration. Who gets into the US? From what parts of the globe are they allowed in from? And how many from each country get to come in? To say that we are a nation of immigrants is trite beyond imagination. Having said that, as a people, Americans have resisted every wave of immigration to hit their shores. Once the English Puritans landed on the East Coast in the 1600s, every ethnic group after that was viewed as interlopers trying to take US wealth and destroy the American way of life. Irish, Italians, East Europeans, the Chinese were all resisted, demonized, and made scapegoats for anything going wrong within the country even as they arrived. The US would not be the country it has become without immigrants as they have always contributed greatly to the economy by providing labor for factories, innovation for industries, and demand for US markets.

The US is struggling with the "immigration problem" again. The economic implications of the current wave of immigrants from Mexico is huge. This group has become the mainstay of labor in many sectors of the US economy. As laws tightening restrictions on Mexicans coming into the US were implemented, several states found themselves struggling to find labor to do much of their agricultural and related work. The service sector, significantly the hotel industry, has come to rely largely on Hispanic immigrants to maintain hotel rooms all over the US. The relatively recent wave of immigrants from Mexico, Central America, and the southern hemisphere has provided ridiculously cheap labor to large swaths of the economy. Yet debate rages on about how to keep them out of the country, in what controlled way to allow some to assimilate into the economy, and what price will be exacted for whatever course is chosen. We are seeing a scenario rerun that has been played out many times in US history.

Consider just a few of the attacks on immigrant populations over history. The Chinese Exclusion Act of 1882 prohibited immigration of Chinese laborers in the US for ten years. In Wisconsin, the Bennett Law of 1890 forbade recognition of any public or private elementary or high schools teaching in languages other than English. An attack on the German-teaching Lutheran and Catholic parochial schools removed their eligibility to satisfy the state's compulsory school attendance law. Chinese immigration was made permanently illegal in 1902. Deportation of 600,000 Mexicans included US citizens between 1930 and 1940 (Adams, et al., 2007). The assimilation of waves of immigrants has tremendous implications for US society, not the least of which are the economic impacts.

No single formula exists for the way each immigrant group works its way into the American society and economy. In the 1860s, the Irish could gain citizenship by volunteering to fight for the North in the Civil War (Samito, 2009). While that creative thinking of the 1860s is not likely to be repeated, whatever rules are written, whatever hurdles are placed in immigrants' paths, whatever penalties are exacted, they will be completely contrived and totally arbitrary. The rules that govern the US economy are created in the minds of men.

Having established, or hopefully at least, planted seeds of doubt in the minds of classical economists that the rules on the box top of this game of economics are, in legal parlance, largely arbitrary and capricious, we come back to an earlier question: Does the system people have created work? Is it producing outcomes that Americans would like to see changed? What criteria should be used to test whether people are getting good results from their economy? Such complex questions are without easy answers, particularly that last one.

We can probably achieve consensus around some rough metrics with which to measure the economy that can support conclusions that the economy is: a) delivering about what we want, or can at best expect, b) failing miserably, or c) at least leaning in one of these directions or the other. Ignoring the philosophical and moral underpinnings for the metrics used to grade the economy, most people in the United States and the developed Western world can probably agree that there are five things that everyone should have in some reasonable minimal amount: (*Human Rights Here and Now*, 1999)

1. Healthy and adequate nutrition
2. Safe, affordable housing
3. Good medical care
4. Opportunity for a good education
5. Opportunity to earn a living and support a family through justly compensated work

These five basic rights of life arguably flow in the US from the simple words in the Declaration of Independence stating that everyone has a right to "life, liberty, and the pursuit of happiness." There is some dispute about whether these fundamental building blocks of a good life are all rights protected by law, but courts in the US have addressed all of them to varying degrees. The trajectory of the legal arguments in the US and internationally suggests a reason to consider these qualities as "rights" to which every person in entitled.

Should the market be responsible for delivering, or attempting to deliver, a quality of life defined by the five noted attributes? There may be disagreement about this, defined by how one answers the following question: Do people exist to serve the market or does the market exist to serve the people? Opting for the latter answer, we must then ask, How well is the market doing in creating and distributing these five core attributes of a good quality of life to all citizens? Are these attributes generally enjoyed by most people? Is the system in place to at least offer the opportunity for most people to realistically aspire to these core attributes?

Healthy and Adequate Nutrition: In the most well fed, arguably overfed, country on the globe, food insecurity (hunger) is a continual problem in many parts of the country. Poverty and food insecurity correlate directly. Food insecurity is most prevalent in the parts of the country where poverty is greatest. The largest group of people suffering from food insecurity are children. Some of the facts regarding food insecurity in the US (USDA, 2019):

- In 2018, 4.3 percent of US households had very low food security. In the more severe range of food insecurity, food intake of some household members was reduced and normal eating patterns were disrupted at times during the year due to limited resources.
- Children were food insecure at times during the year in 13.9 percent of households with children. While children are usually shielded by their parents (who go hungry themselves) from the disrupted eating patterns and reduced food intake that characterize very low food security, both children and adults experienced instances of very low food security in 0.7 percent of households with children (274,000 households) in 2014.
- The prevalence of food insecurity varied considerably from state to state. Estimated prevalence of food insecurity in 2013–15 ranged from 8.5 percent in North Dakota to 20.8 percent in Mississippi.

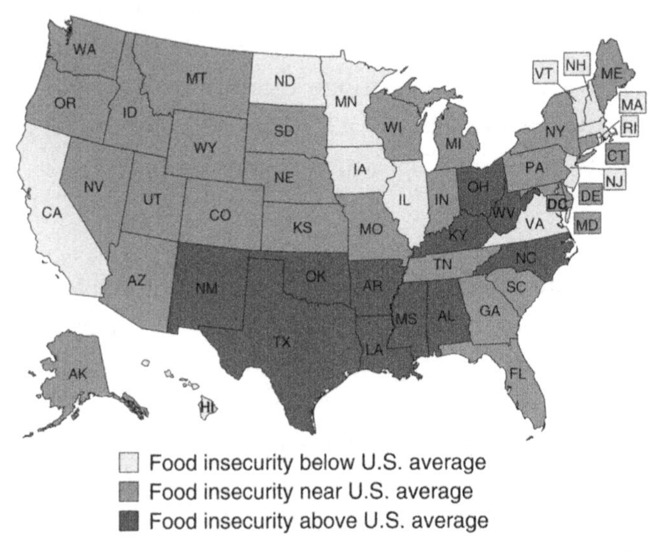

Source: USDA, Economic Research Service using data from the December 2017, 2018, and 2019 Current Population Survey Food Security Supplements.

Figure 1. Prevalence of food insecurity, average 2017-19

- For households with incomes near or below the federal poverty line, households with children headed by single women or single men, women and men living alone, and Black- and Hispanic-headed households, the rates of food insecurity were substantially higher than the national average.
- About 59 percent of food-insecure households in the survey reported that they had participated in the previous month in one or more of the three largest federal nutrition assistance programs: SNAP, Special Supplemental Nutrition Program for Women, Infants, and Children (WIC), and National School Lunch Program. (World Hunger, 2018)

In the 2014–2015 school year, 21.5 million low-income children participated in the National School Lunch Program on a typical day. These are students on the free or reduced-price lunch program. More than 21 million students come from families with such low incomes that a free, or almost free, lunch at school is an important part of their daily nutrition.

Hunger and inadequate nutrition are a nagging problem in the US, but the numbers on the global scale are staggering. Large numbers of people in the US do not have enough to eat. Much larger numbers of people in other parts of the globe suffer from inadequate food supply. Given this fact, the next questions are obvious and simple: is there just not enough food to go around? And if so, are there natural constraints on producing enough food to feed everyone? No. And no.

The undeniable conclusion among agronomists, scientists, and most experts on the agriculture system is that we are currently able to provide enough food to feed the planet today. Certain demographic and weather trends could change tomorrow, but today the planet has adequate food supplies.

The economic system is the framework that manages the production and distribution of, among other things, food. But it does not seem to be working very well. Some areas have food surplus, while others are deficient. Obesity exists alongside hunger. Biodiversity in the US food supply has diminished (OECD, 2019). Agriculture in the United States has become a corn-based system. The US burns almost half of its corn feedstocks in automobile engines; a protein-laden food stock that could be used to feed livestock around the globe. These things point to problems or dysfunctionalities in the system. We should be producing more healthy food. More acres should be going to fruits and vegetables, not feedstock for corn syrup and ethanol. Peoples' health should not be compromised by poor nutrition. We should expect more and better from an economic system that is rationing food in the US and around the world.

Safe Affordable Housing: Everyone should be able to live in safe and affordable housing whether it is owned or rented. Housing meeting those two basic criteria is becoming more elusive for more and more Americans. While the shortages of affordable housing are found all over the country, the problem is more pronounced in some areas than others. Large metropolitan areas on both coasts have some of the greatest housing shortages of anywhere in the country.

Home ownership for most low-income people is nothing more than something they read about in the newspaper or envision watching TV shows. Home ownership is beyond their reach for several obvious factors: lack of savings to make a down payment, unstable income stream, lack of a high-enough credit rating to qualify for a mortgage. Low-income people thus end up in the rental market. Many impediments to finding safe and affordable rental housing face those who are in the rental market. The amount of rental housing available to low-income and very low-income people is very constrained. The widely accepted guideline is no more than 30 percent of income should be spent on housing. In most states, the necessary wage to afford a two-bedroom apartment is above the national or state-mandated minimum wage; in some states on the East and West coasts, it is well above the minimum wage.

The US Department of Housing and Urban Development (HUD) online magazine lays out the problem with affordable housing. The old rule that families who pay more than 30 percent of their income for housing are considered "cost burdened" and "may have difficulty affording necessities such as food, clothing, transportation, and medical care" is an arbitrary oversimplification. An estimated twelve million renter and homeowner households now pay more than 50 percent of their annual incomes for housing. A family with one full-time worker earning the minimum wage cannot afford the local fair-market rent for a two-bedroom apartment anywhere in the United States." (*PD&R Edge*, 2014)

A household with two wage earners earning the minimum

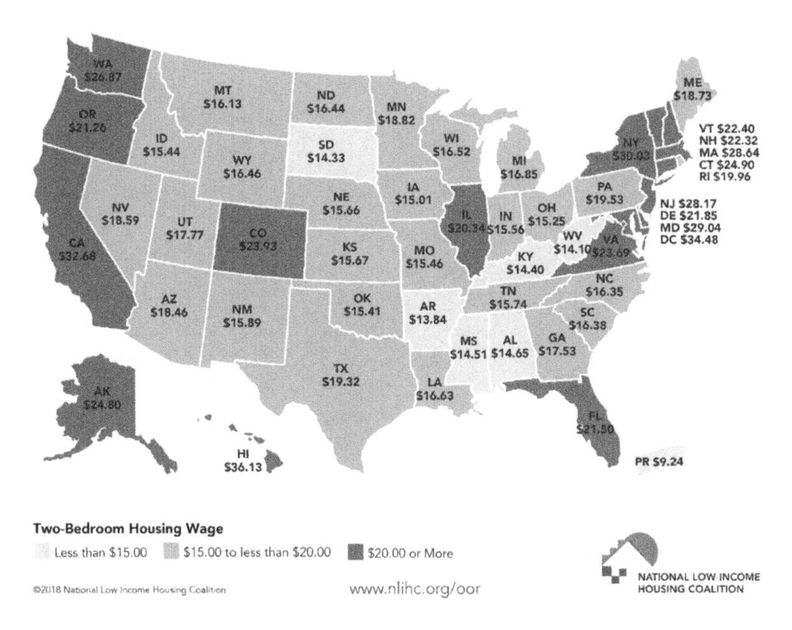

Figure 2. Wage needed to afford two-bedroom apartment by state

wage would be hard pressed in most places to afford a decent two-bedroom apartment. Two people earning the minimum wage would make about $30,000 per year. With 30 percent of their income going to rent they would spend $9,000 per year or $750 per month for rent. There are few, if any, urban areas in the United States where a person can rent a decent two-bedroom apartment for that amount of money (JCHS, Harvard, 2011).

There are market-driven reasons that this is the situation vis-à-vis housing in the United States. While wages for most people have stagnated over the past few years, the cost of housing has continued to rise. Over twelve million households, both owners and renters, are paying way too much for housing, if they can pay for it at all. For a large number of American households, the reality is that wages are too low, and the cost of housing is too high.

People making plenty of money keep builders busy constructing houses and apartment buildings that are out of reach for so

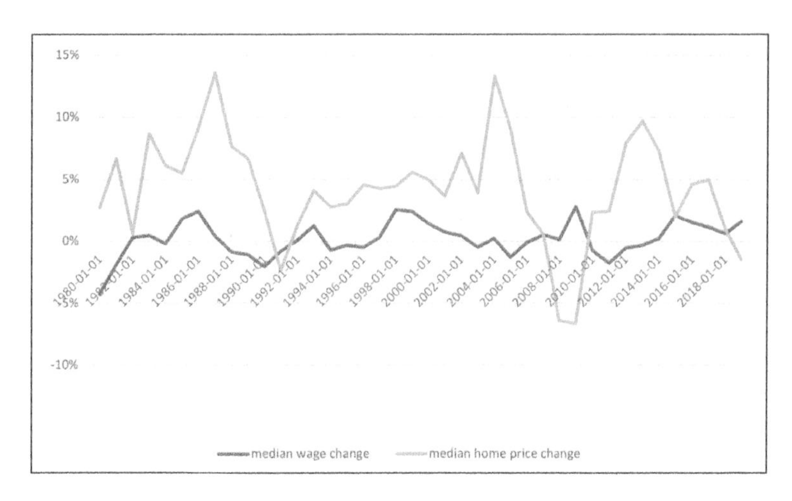

Figure 3. Change in median home prices v. change in median wages

many low-income people. At the same time, many people earn sufficient money to bid the prices on existing housing units up to levels that are out of reach for moderate and low-income people. The US market mechanisms have not done a particularly good job of keeping the supply and demand for housing balanced across all income levels.

Good Medical Care: Of the five indices of success or failure of the US economic system, medical care probably offers the most glaring example of market failure. The failure resides not only in the United States but in many countries around the world. The disparities intra-nationally and internationally in the levels of healthcare are vast. Just look at the realities of healthcare in the US and around the globe:

- The United States spends almost twice as much per capita on healthcare as any other nation yet we rank twenty-first in most categories of healthcare in the Western world (Gramer, 2017).

- Medical science and technology now allow most major organs to be replaced, transplanted, and soon in some cases to be grown in a dish in a laboratory, all accessible if you have good insurance and/or sufficient wealth, yet every year thousands of people die in the US from heart disease that could be prevented if they had access to good medical care (Center for Disease Control, 2020).
- Cancer research and treatment in the US is moving in the direction of studying an individual's genes to determine the genomes related to various types of cancer and the best treatment to cure or to contain it, to develop a treatment tailored to the individual, yet 100,000 people die every year in Africa from malaria. Tuberculosis and polio are still scourges in several African and Asian countries, diseases we have not seen in the United States in fifty to one hundred years.

Advances in medical science are coming about at an ever-increasing rate and the advances themselves are astounding. Yet the distribution of that technology and care is woefully inadequate. Millions of people die every year in parts of the world from diseases and maladies that other parts of the world have not seen for decades and in some cases for a century. Questions abound again. What is it about the US economic system that keeps pushing the boundaries of medical technology further yet so distorts the distribution of that technology that life expectancies among different socioeconomic groups are vastly different? Healthcare in the US is strongly interconnected to healthcare around the world for several reasons, not the least of which is the important role that the US plays in the development of new medical and pharmaceutical technologies. Many advances in medical science come from the US. To a large extent, the healthcare issues that gain priority globally are those that rise to the top in the United States.

In 2011 per the United Nations World Health Organization (WHO), the life expectancy in Japan and Switzerland was eighty-three years; in the United States, seventy-nine years; and in much of Africa, only fifty to fifty-five years. As recently as 2015, the CDC reported the life expectancy for African Americans was more than three years less than for Whites. Many sociological factors cause this discrepancy, but the distribution of healthcare cannot be discounted. According to the US Census Bureau in 2018, 5.4 percent of Whites did not have health insurance; 9.7 percent of Blacks were uninsured, and 17.8 percent of Hispanics were uninsured (Berchick, et al., 2019).

These numbers arise from a variety of factors, but the US market-based system, which distributes, i.e. rations healthcare, plays a large part. Although the US spends more in total dollars and more per capita on healthcare than any other country, the outcomes seen in the US do not reflect this level of expenditure. Life expectancy in the US in 2020 left the country ranked 35th in the world (UN Human Development Report, 2019). Again, this is after spending far more than any other country in the world on the US healthcare system.

Figure 4 shows very clearly what an extreme outlier the US is in terms of its spending on healthcare. The US has no close second in terms of total per capita spending in healthcare. More dramatic than the total US spending on healthcare may be the way in which it is distributed. Private spending on healthcare (private pay or insurance covered payments) are almost exactly equal to public spending on healthcare. This is highly anomalous. Almost all Organization for Economic Cooperation and Development (OECD) countries have a much higher percentage of healthcare paid for by the public sector. Is everyone else wrong and the US is

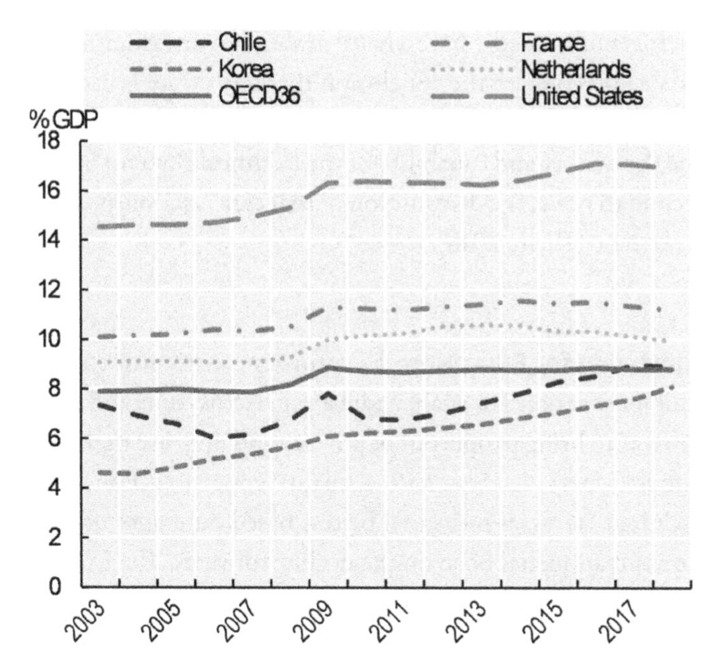

Figure 4. Health expenditures as share of GDP. *Source: OECD Health Statistics 2019*

right? Did France, Germany, Norway, Japan, Canada, and Austria all get it wrong and the United States figured out the best way to provide for healthcare? The health outcomes found in all these countries would argue that is not the case.

The percentage of expenditures coming from the public sector may change over time as the Patient Protection and Affordable Care Act (Obamacare as it is popularly known) becomes more ingrained in the US healthcare structure—providing it remains intact. The data makes the compelling argument: in the US with a healthcare system largely operating in the private sector (market based), the outcomes produced seriously lag behind countries that do not leave healthcare largely in the hands of the market.

Healthcare outcomes differ significantly in the US for Whites and people of color: cancer survival rates, obesity, incidence of diabetes, deaths from childbirth related causes, longevity. A variety of factors undoubtedly have a hand in this, but one cannot analyze the data and come to the conclusion that healthcare is distributed evenly across the population. This again points to the fact that while the quality and capability of the healthcare system in the US is second to none, the distribution of that care is seriously deficient (Hostetter & Klein, 2018).

Opportunity for Education: The primary contributor to a better life for most people is a quality education. Across time and borders, a sure way to bring people out of poverty and improve their quality of life is to provide them with a quality education. Education in the United States, as measured by test-based outcomes of the student population, has been on the decline for years. The US ranked three in the world by some indicators in student achievement as recently as 2000. The US has now dropped to 23rd in the world behind not only most of the developed world but many developing countries as well (Pew Research Center, 2017). This raises serious concerns and questions about what is happening to education in the US on a macro scale. Why are American students steadily falling behind their peers all over the world? At a time when everyday life is becoming more technology driven, production more automated, and all types of machinery more computerized, what does this portend for the United States in its role as the world leader economically and technologically? Where is this going to leave the United States in relation to the rest of the world as the twenty-first century moves forward?

The second indisputable fact about education in the US is that it is delivered very unevenly across the population when analyzed through the lens of student outcomes. The much-discussed achievement gap between White students and Black students, and between White students and Hispanic students, remains dramatically large, greater in some states than others but large in all states.

The data indicates the achievement gaps have shrunk somewhat over the past forty years but remain quite large. Volumes have been written about the root causes of these achievement gaps between segments of the population and proposed strategies to close those gaps. Teachers are underpaid in the US relative to other professions and relative to teachers in other countries. The teaching profession does not hold the status that it should as a career in the US. The teaching profession is held in much higher regard in many other countries, particularly many of those that outperform the US in student achievement. A study in 2016 found that the top twenty-five hedge fund managers earned about 1.5 times the combined income of all of the kindergarten teachers in the US (Yglesias, 2016).

The list of problems acting as a drag on students' performance include large numbers of broken homes, lack of good preschool for many low-income students, lack of opportunity to gain meaningful experiences outside of the neighborhood the child grows up in, and on and on. After all of this has been considered, the greatest correlating factor in student performance is socioeconomic status. Poor students perform worse than more well-off students in most cases. The factors that put a child at risk in education are tightly woven into the characteristics that all too often are tied to low income and poverty, less reading to children while they are young, fewer words spoken to a child during an average day, lack of access to high-quality preschool education, more stress in the daily lives of children, and in the worst cases, lack of good nutrition, medical care, and housing.

The story of education in the US is much like the story of many human rights issues in the US; it has been a slowly evolving process. Education in the late 1700s and well into the 1800s was only afforded to the very well off and only gradually became within sight for people not in the aristocratic class. However, it remained off limits to women until late in the 1800s. Well into the1900s, college education was not the norm for women. The struggle for minorities in the US to gain access to high-quality education has likewise been a difficult and gradual struggle—ironic for a country that was built on wave after wave of immigrants.

The courts have been instrumental, and incremental, in opening the school doors wider for everyone. Brown v. Board of Education (1954) separate but equal education struck down; Green v. County School Board (1968) de facto segregation struck down; Serrano v. Priest (CA, 1971) funding school districts by local property taxes leads to excessive disparities across districts; Force v. Pierce City R-VI School District (1983) failure to allow a girl to try out for the football team violated her Equal Protection rights. Progress made on the legal front has mirrored the gradual progress made more broadly in education being afforded to larger segments of the population. While education has become more accessible to many people, it is still rationed by cost. And the quality of the education offered to and received across segments of society differs greatly.

Opportunity to Earn a Living and Support a Family Through Justly Compensated Work: The most fundamental thing that an economy can provide to people is a job. Jobs are the mainstay of any economy. Jobs are the fulcrum of supply and demand. Work provides the goods and services that are the "supply" of every country's GDP. Jobs create houses, cars, computers, furniture, clothes; they provide medical services, perform accounting functions, prepare food, make movies, and clean hotels. Equally as important, jobs are the essence of "demand." Through the remuneration for work, people have money to spend, which translates into demand for goods and services. A person's eight hours spent making cellphones provides a product to be bought. The income he or she earns becomes demand for food, clothing, and entertainment.

Not only does employment drive both sides of the economic engine, but employment, or lack thereof, has many spillover impacts on the economy and society in general. Unemployment drives up the public cost of social safety nets, correlates highly with crime rates, results in lower levels of healthcare and higher treatment costs, and puts more and more children below the poverty level, which in turn results in lower academic achievement levels. Jobs are not only the fuel for the economic engine but the mortar that holds most elements of society together. Despite the fundamental importance of jobs to an economy, the US has been plagued with the "business cycle" for over two hundred years, and economists still disagree on the underlying causes of this accelerating/decelerating nature of the economy.

There are three fundamental ways in which jobs become problematic to an economy. The first is when there are just not enough jobs for all those who want to work—unemployment. The second problem arises when the quality of the jobs does not match the skill level of those seeking work—underemployment. The third employment problem arises when an individual works full time at a job they want to perform and which society has a need for, but they cannot support themselves or a family with the wage paid—the working poor. This last issue is becoming more common and gaining traction in the press, economic literature, and political discourse. Each of those problems arise from unique, though not unrelated, circumstances. Each causes its own set of problems for individuals and for society.

The US economic system does not have a terribly good track record on any of the employment problems noted above. The period of the Great Depression saw unemployment rates at 15 percent or above for eight years, topping out at 25 percent. World War II brought the unemployment rate down quickly and in large measure.

Until very recently, the structural unemployment rate has been assumed to be around 4 percent. This rate is considered acceptable and results from factors such as people changing jobs. Even if virtually everyone who wants to work has work, there will always be some moving around within the economy as people change locations, jobs, etc. Unemployment has only been in the 4

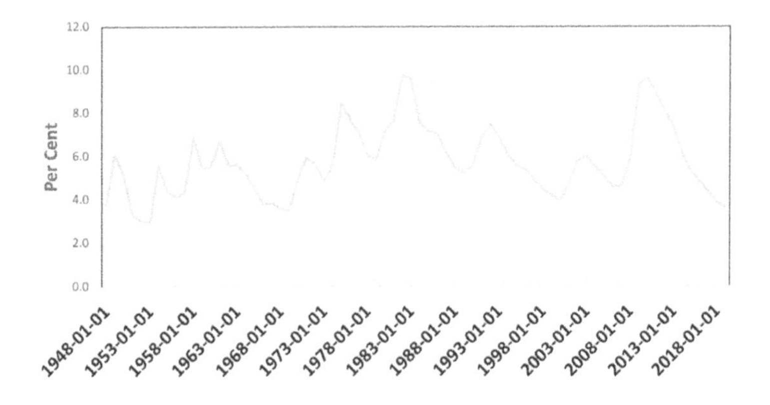

Figure 5. US Unemployment Rate. *Source: U.S. Bureau of Labor Statistics*

percent range, presumed "full employment," for a few years right after World War II, in the late 1960s, and since 2018.

With the onset of the COVID-19 pandemic, unemployment moved well into double digits again and may yet approach levels experienced during the Depression. In recent years there has been discussion among economists as to whether, due to changes in the structure of the US economy; the structural unemployment rate is now closer to 6 percent. Nonetheless, the US economy has struggled in most years to provide jobs for all those wanting to work. The number of jobs created by the economy is half of the problem; the other half is what those jobs pay. Poverty can be spawned by the inability to find a job or by the ability to only find a job that pays too little to support oneself or ones' family.

Figure 6 indicates the official poverty levels for families of various sizes in the US in 2019. A family of four, for example, is living in poverty if they earn below $26,500 per year. Keep in mind what a low bar the federal poverty level sets; what quality of life would the various households below have at the stated poverty levels?

The percentage of people living at or below the poverty level in the US reached 15 percent in 1993 and has been in double digits since then. It has been in the 8 to 9 percent range since 1980. The

Poverty Guidelines for the 48 Contiguous States and the District of Columbia		
Persons in Family/Household	Poverty Guideline	Monthly Income*
1	$12,880	$1,073.33
2	$17,420	$1,451.67
3	$21,960	$1,830.00
4	$26,500	$2,208.33
5	$31,040	$2,586.67
6	$35,580	$2,965.00
7	$40,120	$3,343.33
8	$44,660	$3,721.67
For families/households with more than 8 persons, add $4,540 (annual) for each additional person.		

Figure 6. 2021 Federal Poverty Guidelines. *Source: Federal Register Vol 86, No 19, February 1, 2019.*

---

recession that began in 2007 drove many more people below the poverty level in the US. While that statistic alone is discouraging, a deeper look into those numbers shows that for the past thirty years one-third or more of those living below the poverty line were children. Ironically one of the largest groups of poor people in the US, children, are those that have no ability to do anything to change their circumstances. About 20 percent of children in the US live below the poverty level (Koball, 2018). They can neither get jobs, create jobs, alter the social safety net that prevents them from falling into poverty, nor change the system that prevents their parents from finding work.

The market does not have a particularly good track record in terms of consistently providing an adequate number of jobs that can provide an acceptable level of income for almost all families. There seems to be some serious flaws with Adam Smith's "invisible hand." That invisible hand might be due for serious rehabilitation, if not amputation.

Where Are the Problems in the Economy?

Any argument that the US complex economic system (composed of laws, regulations, Financial Accounting Standards Board pronouncements, social values, time honored "ways of dealing," ingrained cultural leanings) is in any way not the product of the hearts and minds of man is without merit. Borrowing from biology, the economic system did not evolve in any true sense from anything. Borrowing from the law, the preponderance of the evidence suggests that the US system has failed in many of the basic areas from which we should expect more and better results—and more equitable distribution of, jobs, housing, food, medical care, education.

So where do the problems lie and how do we fix them? There are serious flaws in some of the ways we have built this complex system, flaws derived from how parts of the US system have metamorphosed over time, and some major disconnects between how the economic system is designed, is supposed to work, and actually functions. We will focus further on several major components of this system and analyze if we have characterized accurately how they fit into the US system.

Property: For hundreds of years real property was both the primary source of income and the main store of wealth. While the importance of land in producing income and wealth has lessened over time it is still a significant input in many production processes and increasingly becoming a significant component of human well-being. With the world population approaching 8 billion and the space for all of those people fixed at the same level it was when fewer than a million people wandered the earth, the dilemma is clear. People have less and less space in which to live, work, and play. The allocation of that space among people has a significant impact on quality of life and physical well-being.

Demand: The US economic model is based upon consumers making decisions about what they will buy and effectively "voting" for those goods with their dollars. The demand for goods is transferred to producers through consumption expenditures, which information is in turn transferred to and acted upon by producers in creating more of those goods where demand is strongest. Demand drives the economy.

Generally, when supply and demand are well balanced, the US economy works smoothly by most indicators. There will be a reasonably steady amount of growth in the economy, unemployment will be at acceptable levels (full employment), inventories will be at acceptable levels, utilization of resources will be high (capacity utilization), etc. But what really is demand? And how does it get measured in the US economy? When people say the demand for something is high, what do they really mean? And how do we know that is true? These questions are answered in the language of money. Without money, without a medium of exchange, decision-making in the US system becomes rudderless. No signals are being sent from consumers to producers. Without money, the conduit through which information flows through the system ceases to exist. Information is not transferred back and forth between producers and consumers. Query: If half of the people in the world have no money or 15 percent of the people in the US live at or below the poverty line, how are their demands registered within the system?

Flow of Information: One of the fundamental paradigms of the US economic system is that rational people make objective decisions based upon copious amounts of accurate information that guide them in making their economic decisions—the rational man myth. Both the amount and quality of the information available to economic actors is suspect. On the consumer level, arguably most information derives from advertising. Clearly consumer choice is driven by advertising. Can anyone seriously argue that advertising adequately, truthfully informs us? For an indication of the problem associated with the quality of information available to consumers one only needs to look at the legal battles taking place around the US in an arena now referred to as "truth in labeling." With 70 percent of the US economy composed of consumer spending, the makeup of information flowing to consumers has significant import for the economy.

Externalities: As the name implies, this problem is one of failing to capture elements of the cost structure in the US accounting systems that guide decision-making in the production process. Volumes have been written about the problems of externalities, but they never seem to remain for long in the front of the US economic discussions as they should. The failure to deal adequately with externalities in the US system is brought into sharp focus as California burns, Miami and New York City experience regular tidal flooding, the dead zone in the Gulf of Mexico increases annually in size, and payments to families through various social safety nets increase as unemployment decreases.

Measurement: GDP is the yardstick by which we measure the US economy and those of every country on earth. Focus and emphasis is placed on what we measure. If the US educational system is graded on spending per pupil, the focus will shift to costs rather than educational outcomes for students. If healthcare systems compete based upon convenience of location, amenities offered in private rooms, amount of state-of-the-art imaging equipment on site, then look for patient outcomes to get lost in the shuffle. If a corporation's metric is earnings per share (net income divided by the number of shares outstanding), then the corporation's every effort will be focused on raising the numerator or lowering the denominator, e.g. through stock buybacks. Similarly, if the nation's macroeconomic metric is deeply flawed, it will have significant negative implications for economic policy and output. The US collective focus will be diverted from measuring and improving the quality of people's lives toward increasing numbers that may at times actually be harmful to society as a whole.

Income and Wealth Inequality: The skewed distribution of income and wealth varies widely over time within a country and even more widely between countries. Imbalanced wealth distribution is really a byproduct of the factors above (in addition to many other pieces of the US system not discussed in this book). But it is of such great importance that it will be discussed along with other broken parts of the US economic model.

This list of problems with the market model is by no means exhaustive. It does highlight some of the glaring problems that confront the US system. Hopefully it will encourage people, most significantly academics and those setting economic policy, to begin to view the US system from a different perspective and break out of some of the time-honored ways of thinking about the US economic system.

Thus far we have established that the US economic system was not delivered from on high on stone tablets, nor did it crawl on econometric legs out of the primal soup and evolve to what it has become. The great economic engine was built by many architects—some well-intentioned, some not so. We have at least made a cogent argument that the US system has failed in a number of ways and not produced particularly satisfying results. This value-laden statement is discussed in more detail in the next chapter. Suffice it to say that there seem to be enough questions about how evenly quality of life is distributed among the population to warrant some significant fine-tuning if not a complete overhaul. A few of the flaws in the underlying assumptions about the US economic system prevent it from working in the manner it is intended to work, which will be also discussed in more detail. Chapter 1 deals with the way we evaluate the US economic system and the standards to which we should hold it.

CHAPTER 1

EVALUATING THE SYSTEM

Justice: Taking the Dog Out of the Fight

What will likely turn out to be the most valuable future resource, the resource that will change the hierarchy of the haves and have-nots, is knowledge. Knowledge in the abstract sense, and technology in the applied sense, will surpass oil, coal, and minerals of all types as the real determinant of individual and national wealth. In the eighteenth, nineteenth, and twentieth centuries the Western nations went all over the globe in search of natural resources. Developing nations, particularly China and India, have been coming to the developed nations to mine technology. They want to buy it, steal it, deconstruct it, replicate it, make it part of their own economies.

The battlefields upon which the developed nations and the developing nations collide will become fewer and fewer river valleys, mountaintops, and vast desert expanses. The new battlefields will be international organizations such as the UN, the World Trade Organization, and the internet, where the fights will be over intellectual property rights, patent law, copyright infringement, and technology piracy. Conflicts will be fought in cyberspace.

Aggressors with advanced technology will be as feared as those with large numbers of tanks and aircraft.

Nine of the ten largest US corporations in 1965 were oil companies, auto manufacturers, steel and other manufacturing companies. By 2017, eight of the ten largest corporations were internet companies, software companies, and financial entities. Whether wealth is found in physical assets and natural resources or in stores of knowledge, it will be monetized and allocated among people by the US economic system. Markets, however constructed, will continue to value and distribute these assets.

We must think more broadly about how economic arrangements function and why. What was the driving force behind the components of the created system? What was behind each law, each regulation, each commercially related court case, every societal perspective that became woven into the markets? If we choose to attempt to make changes to the system as it exists, what underlying factors must change to facilitate that change? If we do not understand what brought us here, we cannot expect to understand how to go about making changes that move the system in directions other than the one it is currently moving and will move.

As stressed already, this system did not just develop organically over time; it did not result from millions of random events in which the stronger, more robust elements survived much like evolution, nor was it handed down on stone tablets from some higher authority. The system in the United States was built over a period at least dating back to when explorers and settlers first arrived. It grew and changed over time and developed into a much broader and deeper economic and social system; but it did not do so randomly. The US economic system was built brick by brick, and by design. Granted the basics of this system have changed over the course of 200-plus years; but each change, each fine-tuning adjustment made to the system, was done very purposefully by someone. Most if not all steps forward economically come about on the shoulders of work someone in prior times has done. But it is fair to say that when it comes to the US economy writ large, people did build it. Americans built it and would be remiss not to look back once in a while and see if what was built needs some remedial work.

Virtually every transaction that takes place in the US economic system, no matter how small or large, has a value or principle underlying it. If you ask of every transaction, why do we do it that way?—we will discover the foundational principle that guides each transaction. For example, go into a probate court and watch as a decedent's land is passed on to his or her children. US law has determined that once land is acquired, title to the land stays with the person in perpetuity until sold or given away. That has not always been the case over time in other parts of the world. Stand in a teller line at a bank and watch as an unskilled service worker cashes a paycheck for $580 for two full weeks of work. Someone determined that $7.25 per hour was adequate compensation for that individual's work, that $7.25 per hour once set would not be subject to yearly inflation rates, and that the hourly wage would only be revisited seven times in the past thirty years.[1] That is a long time between raises in the US economy.

Turn back the clock to 2006 when some of the most highly compensated people in the country made business decisions that wreaked financial havoc on the economy of the US and most of the world. Their decisions were motivated and allowed by banking and financial industry laws and regulations that shifted huge amounts of risk away from institutions and people running them, and shifted the risk to the government and taxpayers. The laws and regulations that allowed this did not evolve.

Look into the financial calculations that underlie the development and construction of a coal-fired power plant. Tax credits are built into the analysis that encourage power generation; there

1. US Dept. of Labor. History of Federal Minimum Wage Rates Under the Fair Labor Standards Act, 1938–2009.

is a glaring absence of the costs associated with the carbon output of the power plant in the analysis. We highly value the output of energy but are not overly concerned with the downstream costs of its production. The interests of those who sit on the benefit side of the equation are given far greater weight than those who bear the costs of the energy production. The US values are on display in the rules written to guide virtually all commercial interactions, or at least the values of those who have and will participate in the writing of those rules.

Once we accept the idea that we function under certain laws, rules, regulations, practices, and customs because we have ordained that it be that way, we are on the road to understanding the US economic system in a fuller perspective. Questions start to arise around not only where we have arrived with the US economic system but *why* we have arrived at this point. Ancient texts like the Bible, the Torah, and the Koran may speak to what people strive for, or would like to think guide human values; but an equally weighty book, the Internal Revenue Code, tells the true story of where US values lie. There is a unique story behind every chapter, section, and subsection of the IRS code. Someone's economic interest or economic value underlies every part of the tax code. That is not to say there is not a value or judgment behind every law in the federal and state statutes, but the US tax laws represent the complete juxtaposition of commerce and values. The US tax laws clearly depict the thinking and attitudes of the tax writers, and it has changed over time. A look at historical tax rates in the United States illustrates this point.

Up until the time of the Civil War, there was no income tax in the US. The cost of the Civil War brought financial expediency into play with the creation of a two-tier tax rate of 3 percent on income under $10,000 and 5 percent on income over $10,000, which was a large income back in 1863. In 1895 a decision handed down by the US Supreme Court, Pollock v. Farmers' Loan & Trust Co., 157 U.S. 429 (1895), had the effect of making the income tax unconstitutional so no income tax was collected from 1895 until the 16th Amendment was ratified in 1913. This eighteen-year period with no income tax fell during what is referred to as the Gilded Age in the US—a period during which huge personal fortunes were accumulated by a small number of industrialists in the US, Carnegie, Vanderbilt, Getty, and Rockefeller, to name a few. In 1916 the highest marginal tax rate rose from 7 to 15 percent. The following year in 1917, the highest marginal tax rate jumped to 67 percent on incomes over $2,000,000, extremely high income in those days.[2] The huge increase in tax rates was driven by a need to finance the United States war effort during WWI, and driven by the idea that the war should be paid for currently and not by incurring large deficits to be paid off in the future.

In 1919 the highest marginal tax rate went up to 77 percent, and rates stayed high for several years. A value trade off was made in this time period also. Prohibition became the law of the land in 1920; up until then, the excise tax on liquor had supplied much of the revenue for the federal government. Around 1920 the evils of liquor were traded off against the imposition of a higher income tax. From 1925 to 1931, the top marginal rate was reduced to 25 percent.

In 1932 with the Depression taking an ever-larger toll on the US and world economies, the highest tax rate was raised to 63 percent. Increased revenue was needed to fund social programs instituted by Franklin Roosevelt as he fought to pull the country out of the Depression and pull millions of people off soup lines. The onset of WWII saw the top tax rate go up to 94 percent in 1943 and 1944. Economic expediency again caused changes in tax policy. But in the 1940s, America was at war, it had to be paid for, and most people supported the war effort. Top rates stayed in the 90 percent range until 1964 and then dropped back to 70 percent until 1981.

---

2. Internal Revenue Service. SOI Tax Stats-Historical Table 23. 1913–2015.

Income Level	Marginal Tax Rate (Tax Bracket)	Long-Term Capital Gains Tax Rate
$0 to $9325	0 %	0 %
$19,400 to $78,950	12 %	0 %
$78,950 to $168,400	22 %	15 %
$168,400 to $321,450	24 %	15 %
$321,450 to $408,200	32 %	15 %
$408,200 to $612,350	35 %	20 % over $488,850
$612,350+	37 %	20 %

Figure 7. US Income Tax Rates: Ordinary Income and Capital Gains. *Source: Internal Revenue Service*

In 1982 the top rate started its long decline into the 20 and 30 percent rates we have seen over the past two decades. While the appeal by many is to lower tax rates, when viewed in a long historical perspective, current tax rates are quite low when compared to earlier times.

The tax rate on capital gains has undergone similar changes up and down over the years as did the income tax rates on ordinary income, capital gains being the appreciation in value of capital assets over a time period of one year or longer. In recent years, the tax rate on capital gains has been lower than the rates on "earned" income. Figure 7 shows the 2019 capital gains tax rates in effect corresponding to the various ordinary income tax rates for joint tax filers.

The tax rate on "labor" (ordinary income) is higher than the capital gains rate at every income level and almost twice as high at the very top end of the income tax scale. A value judgment has been made that income from labor should be taxed at a much higher rate than income from appreciating assets. Capital gains are "earned" primarily by those in upper-income brackets.

Most capital gains accrue to those in the highest income tax

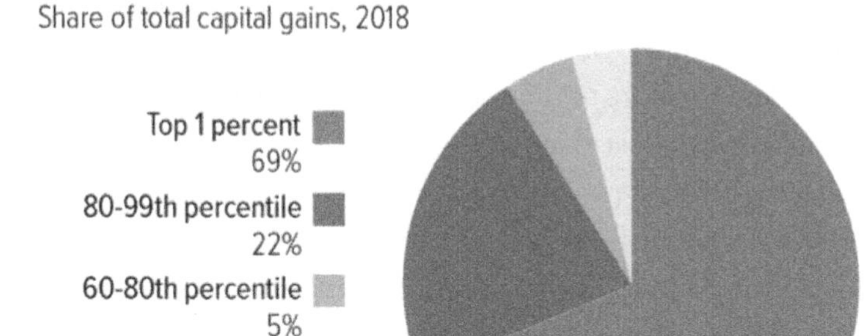

Figure 8. Distribution of Capital Gains by Income Groups

bracket. For a very wealthy individual earning most, or a significant amount, of their income from capital gains, that income is taxed at a lower rate (20 percent) than an individual earning from $38,000 to $92,000 per year (25 percent). In other words, an individual making $19 per hour is taxed at a higher marginal rate on his "earned" income than the capital gains earned by someone whose ordinary income is in excess of $406,000 per year. If the wealthy individual has very little ordinary income, putting them in a lower ordinary income tax bracket, the tax on their capital gains drops to 15 percent. A value judgment? Absolutely. Taxing someone who does hard physical labor forty hours a week at a higher rate than an individual who earns their income by managing and trading securities reflects a value judgment.

This tax discrepancy hides behind the unsubstantiated argument that capital gains add to economic growth and job creation.

When the tax emperor is stripped of his imaginary clothes, the result is a value statement about whose efforts should do more to support the structure of the US economy. It has been determined, at least for the time being, that lower-income earners should contribute relatively more to the common good than those who, arguably, benefit the most from all aspects of the infrastructure and orderly economic system Americans enjoy.

As a further example of how changing values have impacted the structure of the US society, and therefore, the US economy, look no further than education. By the middle of the 1800s, high schools began to appear in many parts of the country but were attended mostly by children of upper-income people. In the beginning of the 1900s and up until the time of WWII, free public high schools were built in large numbers all over the country. The resulting impact on the amount of the population receiving an education was dramatic.

In 1910 less than 20 percent of high school-age children were enrolled in high school, but by 1940 over 70 percent of high school-age children were attending school (Snyder, 1993). The value of education to society as a whole was seen along with the need for an educated work force for the economy. Collectively, the United States determined to make twelve years of education not only available to everyone but in most states compulsory for everyone.

College has remained for the most part something that has to be individually funded—neither required nor universally funded as is high school. However, with the rapid pace of change moving society and economies to more technologically driven systems, the need for increased levels of education is being realized. Discussion is now taking place in parts of the country about the merits of making two years of post-secondary education free to everyone, much as happened with high school a hundred years ago.

The way Americans have built the economy says who we are. It tells what we value—what is most important and what is not terribly important. Do we have an economy we are content with? Is it accomplishing what we want? Is it moving society in the direction we want? What values do we want reflected in the economy that are not present? How do we build those changes into the fabric of the economy, or is it even possible to do so? These questions will be answered differently by most, and the differences may be quite large. Do we strive for consensus on these questions? Does the majority rule? Are some answers to these questions just inherently right and some wrong by almost any standard we use for the metric?

Let's look at some core tenets that should define and guide an economy:

Fairness: Is the US system "fair"? Should it be fair? How does one define fair? Fairness may mean an equality of opportunity but that also raises questions. Everyone starts from a different set of circumstances, at a different time, in a different place, with different talents and attributes. So how do we define "fair"?

Justice: Should the US system be organized so that everyone receives justice? Just outcomes or just opportunities? Can we ever agree on whether justice is being shared throughout the economy?

Improving lives: Does the US system give people the opportunity to improve their lives? Does it provide that opportunity to everyone or just a few? Does everyone, by some measure, receive the same relative tools to improve their lives?

Incentives to innovate and grow the economy: Does the economy effectively encourage people to seek ways to improve processes and products in ways that will either expand economic output or improve the quality of life for oneself and others?

Equitable asset and wealth distribution: How does the economy affect the distribution and accumulation of wealth? If wealth distribution is moving toward greater disparity across the socioeconomic spectrum, is that beneficial? Does growing disparity in wealth distribution happen in spite of, or because of, the way the system is structured?

Legacy for the future: Is economic activity taking into account the welfare of generations yet to come? Is capital of all forms—human, intellectual, physical—being added to or depleted? Are incentives, programs, and systems in place to at least conserve resources if not augment them? Economic activity has both spatial and temporal dimensions.

How are these issues addressed at present? Who or what institutions have the controlling power to shape these discussions and make decisions? In the US, many forces weigh in on the issues set out above. An intertwined web of people and organizations bring change to the market. Political parties, religious institutions, special interest groups, the judiciary, and individuals all have a voice in shaping the US economy. The views and values of all of these constituencies have changed over the years and will no doubt continue to do so.

The polarity of the Republican and Democratic parties has changed dramatically over the years. In the early twentieth century, republicans were the protectors of the land and the party of conservation. That changed significantly by the beginning of the twenty-first century with republicans now more interested in the development of natural resources than the protection of fragile ecosystems. In the antebellum South, the Democratic Party clung to segregation and fought to keep Black people from achieving true equality under the law, voting rights, and property ownership. By the 1960s, democrats were the party advocating for the interests of minorities of all types.

Religions too undergo large philosophical shifts. All major Christian religions in the US are moving, albeit at varying paces, toward greater inclusion of women in roles of responsibility within their hierarchies and greater acceptance of heretofore outcasts like gays. In the Catholic Church, for example, these changes are being led more from the "pew" than the "pulpit."

The makeup of the judiciary has shifted over the centuries from liberal to conservative and back again. The US Supreme Court, federal courts, state courts, often make decisions that have very long-lasting impacts on the US market system. The central tendency of the judiciary changes over time also. For example, the court moved from a liberal composition under Chief Justice Earl Warren in the '70s and '80s to a much more conservative court under Chief Justice John Roberts.

Every economic system by its very nature has a moral underpinning. It distributes a finite amount of resources among people and across generations. Whether its design tends toward allocating resources to the strong, the intelligent, the already privileged, the underclass, or a particular ethnic group, the overall profile of advantage and disadvantage in a society is an accurate barometer of values.

Socialism, as it was developed in the late nineteenth and early twentieth centuries in Europe, developed along purely secular lines to the point of condemning organized religion in the process. Nonetheless, socialism was built around strong moral judgments. Wealthy, resource-laden people were corrupt; wealth was gained by the few on the backs of the masses of underprivileged people; everyone started out with different skills and resources and socialism basically set out to level the playing field. There was a moral correctness in everyone having the same resources. On the other hand, the capitalist system that developed in the eighteenth and nineteenth centuries in Europe and continued to develop in twentieth century America was arguably built upon Judeo-Christian morality as interpreted in the Protestant religions of Europe. Many of the early economic writers came from backgrounds that were influenced strongly by organized religion (Strathern, 2004). This clearly shaped much of the economic thought of the day. Wealth, far from being viewed in a negative light, was seen as resulting from hard work, industriousness, temperance, and keen intellect. "Good" people were favored by God and he in turn allowed them to acquire wealth, a view found in contemporary prosperity theology.

The intense colonization that European nations undertook in the 1700s and 1800s was often justified under the theory that the civilized Europeans were doing indigenous people a favor by forcefully bringing European culture to them. The way of life of indigenous peoples in Africa, North and South America, and Asia was viewed as barbaric, and these savage nations could only benefit from being made to resemble Europeans. This thinking also made it easier to rationalize the brutality visited upon indigenous peoples by the conquerors who conveniently also had higher uses for the natural resources of the conquered lands than did the vanquished people.

If one accepts the proposition that the existing distribution of resources among nations, and between people within nations, is the result of the functioning of everyone's economic systems, and that the further distribution and allocation of resources going forward will be a result of the economic systems under which distribution takes place, then even the ardent secularist must acknowledge that there is a moral element to economic systems. The US economic arrangements reflect values and ethics, if not of society at large at least of those with their hands on the pen writing the rules. There is more to evaluating an economic system than asking whether it is "working" or not. That answer will depend upon where on the income/wealth distribution curve the respondent lies. To someone in the top 1 percent or .1 percent of that curve, the system will unquestionably be deemed as working quite well. For someone in the bottom 20 percent of the socioeconomic spectrum, the economy is probably not working quite so well. This is an incredibly inadequate way to understand the US economic system. The US system needs to pass muster when evaluated against the types of guideposts set out above.

Is the US system fair, just, equitable? These are not easily or well-defined concepts to evaluate. Volumes have been written by philosophers, ethicists, and theologians attempting to describe and understand the nuances of these terms, with a fair amount of disagreement still existing. Yet unless we are willing to content ourselves with rationalizing concepts such as "to the victor goes the spoils," "might makes right," or "luck of the draw prevails," we are compelled to hold the US system to higher standards centered around notions of fairness and justice. How do we do that? What ought we to strive for morally in a macroeconomic sense? What should the US economic systems do? What should they encourage? What type of production should be fostered? And how should the production be allocated? How should resources be managed within generations and across generations? These are the fundamental questions that have always concerned the science of economics.

John Rawls may have been the most significant moral and political philosopher of the twentieth century. In his seminal work, *A Theory of Justice* (Oxford Press, 1973), Rawls deals with broad notions of human society and questions of what basic rights everyone should have in a "just" society. His work is expansive and discusses many areas of society and political systems, but he does spend some time discussing economic arrangements. Rawls defines justice in terms of fairness. That may seem like little more than exchanging one term for another, but a careful reading of Rawls reveals his concept of fairness.

Rawls sets out his notion of fairness by creating a paradigm through which he sets up a just society. Rawls describes a system of distributive justice in the following way: A just system begins from an "original position" in which everyone is similarly situated at the beginning and, as the rules for the system are constructed, those writing the rules operate behind a "veil of ignorance." That veil of ignorance says that none of us knows what our position in life will be, what our personal traits and strengths will be, what assets we may start with. It describes a totally random process for everyone in which chance determines whether we start out with high intelligence, low intelligence, learning disabilities; whether we are born into a wealthy family with two parents or a poverty-stricken single parent family; whether we are gifted with great strength and athletic prowess or suffer severe physical impairment.

Faced with this tremendous uncertainty of where we will start out and what we will start out with, Rawls argues that the rules we construct for a system of justice will tend to be fair, given that we, the creators of the system, will not want to inadvertently stack the cards against ourselves. While Rawls does not talk directly about an economic system with his philosophy, the parameters of his paradigm can be applied to the construction of an economic system. Taking Rawls' ideas on societal justice broadly, and narrowing it to economic systems, provides one framework for viewing and analyzing an economic system.

Rawls does not dismiss the reality of the world wherein all people begin differently, under different circumstances, with varying talents and resources. He deals with this under the concept of his "difference principle." The difference principle is a bridge between the fine theory and the circumstances which actually exist, between developing the system in a time vacuum and actually reworking the system moving forward from today. Rawls' difference principle requires that raising the outcomes of one group in society cannot happen unless the potential outcomes for all groups in society are also raised. In this regard Rawls breaks from the economic theory of maximizing total utility in that his view of justice does not allow one group being made better off if all groups are not somehow also made better off. To do otherwise violates his difference principle and hence his concept of justice. Utility maximization theory just requires that the total sum of utility (however defined) be maximized even if most utility resides in a small portion of the population. It is not concerned with the distribution facets of utility.

Rawls' difference principle also contrasts with the economic concept of "pareto optimality." The principle of pareto optimality states that the economically optimal state is one in which no person can be made better off (i.e. gain utility) without another person being made worse off (i.e. losing utility). If it is possible for someone to gain utility without anyone else's utility being diminished, then there are more optimal allocations of resources that should be employed. Rawls' paradigm argues that increases in "utility" should be spread across all groups at least to some extent. In these regards, Rawls breaks from traditional classic economic principles.

To deal with Rawls' paradigm in the context of the US market economy requires some creative thinking. Remember, the "veil of ignorance" surrounding our "original position" asks us to consider that not only is it a random process that will put us into the early twenty-first century, the late twenty-first century, the early twenty-second century or beyond; but likewise, our original position might have us born in the United States, Germany, India, China, Somalia, or any other part of the world. We do not know where or at what time we will live out our life. Again, not only do we not know where on the globe or at what point in history we will be given the opportunity to live out our life, but we do not know what resources and talents we will begin with. Quick reflection tells us that this is a perfectly accurate description of reality. One constant for all of humanity is the accident of birth. The time and place of our existence and the gene pool we live it with are the result of a seemingly random selection process.

What does this notion of fairness imply for a market-based

economic system? It has implications for analysis within the current generation and between the current and future generations. The concept of economic fairness between generations is taking on greater and greater significance as issues of resource depletion and accompanying environmental degradation take on greater urgency.

Looking at fairness of the economic system between different income strata of the American population, relevant questions are:

> What does the market offer these groups in terms of opportunity?
>
> What would the market offer each strata if fairness prevailed?
>
> If a transition were needed to satisfy notions of fairness, would there be positive economic results? And for whom?
>
> And if "fairness shifts" were made, how would they be best made?

A Rawls Inquiry into the Market . . .

There are more frameworks within which we can evaluate the functioning of the US economy if we choose to look at it through a moral lens. Quite possibly some would simply choose not to look at the economy that way. We might prefer to take a purely secular approach to the US system and what it gives Americans by means of distribution of assets, allocation of costs, consequence of who bears the burdens, and who reaps the benefits. But unless one takes the view that the US market system has naturally and organically evolved, a concept previously discussed, one must take the view that the system has been written over time by people who had the power, position, and interest in doing so. And if the system has worked largely to the benefit of its authors, so be it; the strong, the powerful, the wealthy, and the highly connected get their way. To those taking that view, the legitimizing rationale is: luck of the draw. If I am born on top, I will use my position to remain on top. But even that view of the market is not devoid of moral statements being made by those holding such views.

Choosing at this point to look at the US system through a different lens, what should we choose? Every major religion has much to say about the morals and ethics of how people should treat one another, what constitutes justice, what kinds of institutions foster justice. If pressed, most people will look to the teachings of their religion, if they have one, for guidance as to what constitutes a "good "or "just" economic system. Again the philosopher John Rawls has provided a compelling framework within which to think about the US system. While the extremely detailed discussion of justice in his Theory of Justice is not aimed directly at economics, it is highly apropos. It provides what might be considered a purely secular perspective to apply to the analysis required here. Remember, Rawls' theory has two critical notions applicable to a US market analysis: 1) *an original position*; which states that we will all start out at some place, some time in history, with a set of attributes and circumstances; 2) *a veil of ignorance*; which says that none of us know what time, place, or circumstances we will be born into. Rawls contends that with these ideas as a backdrop, everyone will make much fairer, more equitable choices if they are put in the position of the decision-maker or policymaker constructing or remediating the economic system.

Keep in mind that the authors of the system do not know if they are going to be dropped into the eighteenth century, nineteenth century, twenty-first century, and so on. Similarly, they do not know if they will be inhabiting the resource-rich United States or the resource-poor regions of Saharan Africa. They may be blessed with great intelligence or saddled with a poor intellect, fortunate to have great physical skills and prowess or be burdened with physical defects from birth. This quite simple but an immensely powerful paradigm seeks to level the overriding condition of humanity—accident of birth.

Removing time from the equation, i.e. ignoring intergenerational issues, and leaving geography out of the mix, focusing instead upon just what transpires in the United States, we are still left with a large number of life-shaping factors over which none of us have any control: Are we born White, Black, Brown, some of each? Do we enter in the upper class or lower class or somewhere in between? Does our home offer a stable environment with two loving parents? Or is it a struggling home with one parent burdened with an addiction? Do we have a high-powered intellect? Or will we be consigned to remedial academic situations our entire life? Do we swim in a sea of stable people who provide good examples to us at every turn? Or is our given landscape one of people struggling with poverty and other barriers and barely able to survive?

These are the questions Rawls' paradigm would have us consider. It is devoid of any religious tenets or beliefs, and not built on moral judgments construed by any faith. It is simple and practical at least in its conceptual underpinning. Rawls would say, step behind the veil of ignorance and construct an economic system that you are comfortable with, not knowing anything about where or when you will enter the process or under what circumstances; but be assured you will enter the process in some "original position."

Let us look at a few characteristics of the US economy and see how Rawls' paradigm might cast them in different terms. The tax code is low-hanging fruit for this analysis. Certainly it is one of the most self-interested pillars of the US economy with great implications for individuals as well as influencing market decisions for corporations. As we have discussed, tax rates in the US have moved widely over time and will likely continue to do so. Assuming for the moment that there is some general agreement that tax revenues are needed to support necessary parts of the government and infrastructure such as national defense, roads, waterways, court systems, food safety, fire and police protection, etc., where should the burden for supporting these things fall?

If a person has taxable income of $500,000; $1,000,000; or

$10,000,000 in 2020, they probably prefer the existing top marginal tax rate of 37 percent, or lower if possible. If a person is living on the minimum wage, they likely support the earned income tax credit and the lowest possible tax rate. Now suppose these two individuals step behind Rawls' veil of ignorance to set tax policy. What will tax policy look like? Since the chances of ending up in the top 1 percent are just 1 percent, and the odds of ending up in the lower half of income earners is one out of two, US policymakers may not be too wedded to keeping the top marginal tax rates low and may be more inclined to increase the income level at which the EIC phases out. Certainly, with the far greater likelihood of being in the lower or middle class rather than the upper class, taxing capital gains at lower rates than earned income likely will not happen. If one expects that physical labor will likely be the way one earns a living, giving an advantage to capital gains will not be viewed favorably. To skew the tax code in favor of those in the highest income brackets would require a rational decision-maker to think that his chances of ending up in the highest brackets are themselves quite high and, in addition, if the would-be policymaker ends up in that high income tax bracket, s/he will want to keep things tilted in their favor with relatively low marginal tax rates being one way to do so. But remember, the mathematical chance of being in the top 1 percent of income earners is exactly 1 out of 100.

How about environmental issues, laws, regulations? Environmental degradation, resource depletion, and climate change are extremely critical issues and will continue to be so. Let's look at the practice of mountaintop mining that has been utilized in the Appalachian regions of the United States; a process in which vast swaths of mountaintops are literally removed, and coal or other minerals are extracted from the resulting residue. If you had a reasonable chance of being born in a region of West Virginia where the practice of mountaintop mining is, has been, and might be utilized going forward in this planning exercise, and you had an even chance of being someone who made their living from the physical beauty of the region, tourism for example, as opposed to working in the coal mining industry, you might be adamantly opposed to the practice. You might advocate totally banning the practice. On the other hand, if you had a reasonable chance of becoming an owner, executive, or shareholder of a company that practiced mountaintop mining, or work as a coal miner, you might be quite favorably disposed to the practice. The point is, when we look at present circumstances with everyone having already been placed in their "original position," there is little debate about how the participants will try to write the rules. If these same two people were placed behind the veil of ignorance and told they would be one or the other, how would the rules be written? Quite possibly something vastly different from current rules would prevail. More protection might be given to the mountaintops, more stringent reclamation procedures might be written into the laws. Once we know our circumstances, our views are staked out easily, and we quite rationally tend toward positions that tend to benefit our own given position.

Another high-profile environmental issue concerns hydraulic fracturing of rock to release oil and gas: fracking. Fracking is heavily utilized in many parts of the country to expand oil and gas production. North Dakota, Texas, Pennsylvania, Ohio, New York, and Oklahoma are a few states that are home to a lot of fracking activity. While there are unsettled questions and debate about the practice, some things are becoming more accepted. The process itself puts large amounts of chemicals into the ground which have a likelihood of contaminating groundwater. The process of infusing wastewater back into the ground to fill the voids left after extracting the oil and gas appears to result in an increase in seismic activity in those areas (Oklahoma Geological Survey, 2015). High amounts of air pollutants are released into the air near where fracking takes place.

So how do we write the rules to regulate fracking? And who writes them? As happens in so many sectors of the economy, the industry itself plays a large part in writing its own regulatory laws or has a strong hand in writing the rules. Until 2013, the companies utilizing fracking refused to disclose the mix of chemicals that they were injecting into the ground to fracture the rock. In spite of demands for disclosure about what chemicals might be spilling into the groundwater, the laws in effect did not require it.

Let's take our panel of rule-makers and tell them they may end up with a high-level job with an oil company, a sand mining company, or be a landowner whose property sits atop a large deposit of shale gas or silica sand. Alternatively, the rule-writers may be people raising a young family in an area that sits close to a huge shale oil deposit and also gets their drinking water from wells on top of or nearby the oil deposit. Until these people know which situation they will be placed in, how will they write the rules, the laws, and the regulations? Will more open disclosure about the process be written into the laws? Will more study of the groundwater flows in the area be required prior to extraction of the oil and gas? Will liability be increased should negative impacts develop in ensuing years? Or will profitability and return on investment be favored going hand-in-hand with less disclosure and reduced liability for the drillers?

Once we know on which side of the line "luck of the draw" placed a person, their preferences are probably known. If I end up as a young person raising three small children near a shale deposit in North Dakota, my interests will not line up with the oil company executive living in Houston. Unknown circumstances lead to a different set of calculations than certainty about what cards life has dealt us.

The way Rawls' paradigm might, at least on a conceptual level, be focused on the US economic system is hopefully starting to become clear. Rawls' thinking is also appropriate over different timelines, i.e. intergenerational time frames. Do we extract, deplete, degrade resources (air, water, soil) in order to enjoy cheap food, green lawns, big cars? What if current trends continue and we might be born seventy-five years from today, two generations in the future? Would we construct a system that was a better steward of the air, water, and soil?

Similar questions arise around questions affecting geographic disparities. What global macroeconomic rules will I advocate if I might be born in sub Saharan Africa, a slowly vanishing South Pacific island, or a lawless corruptly governed country in Latin America, rather than the Midwestern United States? As I stand behind the veil of ignorance and my odds of being saddled with any set of circumstances are unknown and unquantifiable, my thinking will change from the status quo. Statistically the odds of any favorable set of circumstances befalling any of us are quite small. The chances of being born in the US versus any other part of the world are less than 5 percent. As of 2015, over 700 million people worldwide still lived on less than $1.90/day (World Bank, 2020). It is easy to lose sight of the fact, if we are living comfortably in the United States, just how small the odds were that we ended up where we did. Anyone born in the United States or another highly developed country "won a lottery" at birth, at least in so far as their odds of living a decent life are far greater than those born into Third World countries.

To make one last connecting link between individual circumstances and the economic rules we write, we will apply Rawls' paradigm to slavery. While slavery has known no geographic boundaries, look at it as an economic reality in the United States. Approximately twelve million people were sold into slavery from Africa between the 1700s and 1860. The majority of these slaves were sold in Caribbean Islands or in South America. Several hundred thousand were sold directly in the United Sates over this period. By 1860, when slavery was being dismantled by the Civil War, almost four million slaves were in the US which, at the time, had a population of thirty-one million people; one in thirteen people—a large number of slaves given the population.[3]

---

3. University of Virginia Library. Distribution of Slaves in United States History.

Let us step behind the curtain again and ask, how will you write the laws regarding slavery if you have a high likelihood of being born Black in Africa in the eighteenth and nineteenth centuries? How will you write the laws if you are a White plantation owner in the southern US or a businessperson who benefits from cheap labor? For argument's sake, let us assume you had a one in ten chance of being born Black in Africa during this time period. Would you allow Black people to be treated as property rather than people? What if your chances of being born a White landowner in the United States were even smaller, for example, 1 in 100 or 1 in 10,000, probably more realistic? Would the economic benefits of institutional slavery be so enticing as to outweigh a much higher risk of being a slave rather than a slave owner? Likely not. Evaluating this decision in terms of expected value, as many investment decisions are evaluated, the probability of ending up a slave multiplied by the negative consequences, a life of hell, would far outweigh the outcome of multiplying slave owner odds times the economic benefits of being a slave owner. Who wrote the rules? The laws were written from the safety and certainty of knowing one's place in life, not from the uncertainty of possibly being on the bad end of the transaction.

A Rawlsian construct places everything into the unknown and places everyone on a level playing field. You have the same chances as the person on your left or right of being placed into a set of advantageous or disadvantageous circumstances with respect to a point in history, place on the globe, family, community, individual characteristics—everything that makes a person who he or she is. Given this reality, we are then asked to do what we think is right, fair, and just, tempered not by any particular moral or religious tradition but by how we would like to end up. This is a powerful yet simple framework in which to evaluate the US economy. Do not consider where you are, but rather look at all of the places you might have ended up or where your children might end up, forgetting for a minute the reality that where your children end up is largely controlled by where you end up.

It is not an easy task to apply Rawls' paradigm to the process of writing the rules going forward. It is easier to write "just" rules if the original position is that point in time when all rules are first being written, not two or three hundred years into the process. But it is not impossible to apply Rawls' concepts midstream. Any time we are going to make fundamental changes to the economic system—change tax policy, amend rules and regulations covering collective bargaining, tighten or loosen regulatory oversight of financial markets, alter laws dealing with low-income housing or zoning regulations affecting high end housing developments, place large tracts of land or ocean off limits to commercial development, change environmental regulations dealing with air and water pollution—a series of questions need to be asked and answered. We need to ask what happens to those on both ends of these issues and to those scattered in between. It requires the decision-makers and policy-drafters to ask: How would I view this issue if I were sitting behind this "veil of ignorance" and did not know with any certainty how this position would affect me? Would I support it? Would I oppose it? Would I rewrite it?

While applying Rawls' perspective to actual legislating and policymaking is not easy, the major shift required from the way in which we continue to cobble together our economic system is to leave personal self-interest at the door. Those with pen in hand, writing the rules, be they statutes, regulations, or judicial decisions, need to slip into many different pairs of shoes before putting ink to paper.

To move toward "fair" outcomes in economic arrangements, we must ask a series of questions as we evaluate each incremental change to the structure:

Who will benefit from this change?

To whose detriment will this change work?

How many people will be benefited and how many will be negatively affected?

What will be the size and nature of the benefits flowing to those affected positively?

What will be the size and nature of those affected negatively? Can those negative effects be mitigated?

Is there some way in which benefits of this change might be shared somewhat across all groups?

Will the benefits accruing to those advantaged by the change have any positive impacts for those not directly benefited?

If I did not know my current station in life, how would I evaluate the proposed changes?

Let's walk through this process, not in the abstract, but with a real economic issue. Over the past several years, there has been discussion about the excess methane released into the atmosphere at the wellheads where fracking is used to extract natural gas from underground deposits and from leaky pipelines. Most of this methane is "flared" at the wellhead, i.e. burned rather than captured, or allowed to dissipate in the atmosphere if leaking from pipelines. Regulations have been promulgated to limit and capture the released methane. Subsequently those regulations have been threatened with repeal. Solid data supports the fact that a significant amount of methane gas is released at wellhead sites. The US Environmental Protection Agency cites significant scientific data suggesting that methane is far more harmful than carbon dioxide in trapping heat in the atmosphere thus contributing to global warming.[4] Technology exists to capture the rogue methane gas

4. US EPA. Greenhouse Gas Emissions Understanding Global Warming Potentials.

at the wellhead, but it costs money to install. New methane capture processes are being developed, but the commercially viable processes are expensive (Warner, et al., 2015). Finding and sealing leaking joints in pipelines will also cost money. Let us step behind the veil and think about how this regulation will affect economic arrangements.

Accepting the science behind methane release into the atmosphere, those who benefit from the sequester of methane are essentially those who must live within the atmosphere, i.e. at a minimum, all Americans since it will serve to help mitigate global warming. That would be a good thing for all people in the country. What is the downside to such regulatory control? There will be costs to install and run any equipment that will utilized to capture the methane. Initially the costs will be borne by the drillers and the oil industry. On its face, the cost of producing a gallon of oil or a million cubic feet of natural gas will increase slightly. That will potentially reduce profits. Those affected by decreased profits will be shareholders in the companies affected, and possibly to an extent the senior managers who may see bonuses and/or incentive stock compensation decrease slightly. Very quickly the added costs associated with methane capture may be passed on to the consumers of natural gas. Were that to happen, large numbers of natural gas users might see some small incremental increase in their natural gas bills, though the costs spread over a very large customer base would likely not add more than few cents per unit of gas burned. A fair assumption would be that most gas company executives would oppose such measures and they might be joined by the majority of stockholders in the companies affected. An equally fair assumption is that the vast majority of Americans, believing in the risks of global warming, would see benefits to pulling methane out of the atmosphere and probably not quibble with a few cents to a few dollars of increase in the price of natural gas. The cost borne by each individual would be quite small.

Now envision the policymaker stepping behind the veil of

ignorance, not knowing where circumstances have placed them, and ruling on this issue. S/he would evaluate the likelihood of being one of the large shareholders in an affected energy company as being quite small, even smaller the likelihood of being a top executive at an affected company. The policymaker would likely see climate change as affecting them quite negatively in the near term. As the policymaker considers the possibility of ending up one or two generations in the future, or having children and grandchildren living in those future generations, climate change issues loom even larger.

The policymaker searching for "fairness" will raise their hand for methane sequester. They will do this because they will see it in their objective best interest. They will do so because a rational determination will be that sequestering methane will benefit them now and in future generations. The near-term economic benefits of failing to trap methane has a very small chance of being enjoyed by our policymaker. Thinking in terms of one's self-interest results in a fair decision when one is not blinded by seeing exactly the circumstances life has handed each of us.

Now we begin to think about the US economic system in a different way, possibly a more just way. Much more study needs to be devoted to the existential economic issues raised herein. Depending upon the direction one's ethical compass points, failure to devote significant resources to the study of these issues can be viewed at worst as a moral failure, at best a badly missed opportunity.

One of the very fundamental differences between the hard sciences and the social science of economics is that the former is descriptive (arguably this may be changing), while economics can be prescriptive. For example, physicists have studied light for hundreds of years and continue to unlock new secrets; light is now understood to be part wave and part particle. But light behaves the way it always has even as we have learned more about its characteristics. Scientists study the atom, unlock its secrets, and experiment on ever-smaller particles that make up the atom. But the behavior of the atom, once it is split, cannot be changed. Not so with economics. Not so with "the market."

The rules which govern US economic transactions were penned by people, not some higher, unknown author. When the sun goes down, we might curse the darkness, but we cannot make the sun reappear until it naturally finds the horizon the next morning. If we determine that the economic system is not allocating resources in ways we think it should, we can change it. If the market is not creating the incentives that ought to be there to move individuals and societies in better directions, we can change that. Laws can be passed, regulations can be promulgated, values and mores can be taught and fostered. Economics is a science with extraordinary power to change the human condition and move the "arc of history." The laws of physics, chemistry, and biology have been given to us; the rules of the market we have foisted upon ourselves.

CHAPTER 2

PRIVATE PROPERTY

The Founding Fathers Had Second Thoughts

"I set out on this ground which I suppose to be self-evident, 'that the earth belongs in usufruct to the living;' that the dead have neither powers nor rights over it. The portion occupied by an individual ceases to be his when himself ceases to be, and reverts to the society . . . and the present holders, even where they or their ancestors have purchased, are in the case of bona fide purchasers of what the seller had no right to convey."

—Letter from Thomas Jefferson to James Madison
September 6, 1789

One of, if not the most, basic foundation upon which our economy sits, is private property. Private property is one of those concepts that we think can only exist in one way, the way we have understood it in this country for over 200 years. There is more behind the idea of private property than we realize. Even Thomas Jefferson had second thoughts about how we deal with private property almost 250 years ago. There is more than one way to think about it just as there is more than one way to measure an economy than by GDP. Since property rights are fundamental to a market economy, inequities in how land is divided up and allocated can quickly spill over into inequities in the entire market. We will explore private property in more detail and dig into the underpinnings of how private property has developed, how early thinking has become set in stone. The purpose here is to prod us to continually ask, why?

The notion of private property is an ancient concept, or so it seems. Private property, in one form or another, has existed for over 2,000 years. While this might make the concept of private property seem very ancient, the concept is in its infancy when viewed against the age of the land that the ownership purports to assign to someone. The land pre-dated the concept of private property by eons. Various notions of private property, as defined both legally and economically in different parts of the world, have developed and changed over the centuries to reflect the changing rules of societies and the economic expediencies of the time. Here we will analyze private property in terms of the concept we have developed over 200 years in the United States of America.

The legal system in the US provides an analytical framework within which to think about private property. The legal system in the United States divides private property into two types. There is *real property*, that is, land and most things below it. Then, there is *personal property* or "chattels," the legal term. So real property is essentially land and permanent attachments thereto, e.g., buildings. Personal property is everything else—chairs, cars, patent rights, intellectual property, items attached to real property that can be removed without material damage to the real property, etc.

The distinction between real property and personal property is important from several standpoints. The genesis of the two types of property is vastly different. The origin of all real property dates back in terms of geological epochs. One might say that when the big geological cataclysmic shifts in the earth subsided and the tectonic plates stopped wandering hither and yon, real property was created, land in the sense that we understand it and, in the locations we find it on the globe. Personal property, of course, is a relatively short-lived thing. An important distinction between personal property and real property is that personal property in almost all instances is man-made. Personal property has a creator. Real property, depending upon your religious persuasion, does or does not have a creator; but if it has a creator, the creator's name does not appear in court documents.

The second notion that can be taken from the US legal system that is useful in thinking about ownership of property is the concept of *chain of title*. Chain of title is, as the name suggests, the notion of being able to trace the ownership of property, whether real or personal, from a given point in time back through the successive ownership of individuals as far back as one might care to trace ownership, or as far back as a credible chain of title might exist. For example, the automobile is probably one of the most ubiquitous types of personal property in existence. The chain of title on automobiles is traced through a recording system run by a department of motor vehicles within a state government. When one buys a car from an individual, he is given a piece of paper that tells him that the person he purchased the car from was the prior owner. The individual that he is buying the car from went through a similar transaction possibly with an owner prior to him. One could trace the ownership of the car back to an original owner who bought it from, let's say a General Motors dealer back in 1975, when the car came off the assembly line, was shipped to the dealer and was first sold.

The chain of title is just the legal string of owners of the property from its inception to its most current owner. A similar concept with chain of title exists with real property as well. With real property the recordation system and the tracking of the chain of owners is accomplished through very structured recording systems that have been developed in the United States over the last 250 years. A person can go to a courthouse in any jurisdiction and trace the chain of title on a piece of property back in time over decades and, in some cases, back to the early 1700s when supposed ownership of the property was granted by King George or other divinely named person and without consideration of who was using said property before a foreign interloper decided to grant ownership to a favored individual or individuals. At some point the chain of title will finally end or, at least, become very unclear as to where prior ownership traces from, the usual impediments being the late eighteenth century, the notion of the divine rights of kings, and the Atlantic Ocean.

When one thinks about the chain of title on personal property and real property, the vastly different characteristics of the two kinds of property quickly become apparent. With very few exceptions, all personal property can easily be traced back to its origin at which point someone designed it, built it, and manufactured it; somebody put the boards, the metal, and the components together and created the thing. The builder, the manufacturer, the songwriter, the writer, the creator of the source code was the first owner of the property, and it was within the purview of the owner to put the property into the stream of commerce as s/he saw fit.

Real property on the other hand is quite different. Real property within any time frame relevant to mankind always existed. No one can lay claim to being its creator, at least no one who is ever going to show up in a court of law to defend title to it. Real property has an origin very different from personal property, and therefore all of the issues surrounding title to real property (economic, moral, legal) must be viewed quite differently from the manner in which we think about personal property. Nonetheless, chain of title is the pathway by which we arrive at the determination of ownership, and that is what makes the concept of chain of title noteworthy.

Let us trace back the chain of title on a piece of property for illustrative purposes just to see where that journey leads us. Take a hypothetical 100-acre tract on which a small manufacturing facility is located now. Walk backward chronologically and see how the ownership of this land shifted over time. We will assume this land is in the western part of Massachusetts near the city of Springfield. The current owner, the Acme Company, produces widgets. The Acme Company purchased the piece of property in 1975 from the farmer who owned the property dating back to 1925. As an aside, this piece of property, which used to be in a more rural area, was annexed by the City of Springfield in 1965 as the City developed and grew out to abut the farmland. The last of the property stayed in agricultural production until it was sold to Acme in 1975. Farmer Brown and his family purchased the farmstead in 1925 from the Goodfellow family who farmed the land from 1825 until 1925 when they fell upon hard times and had to sell the farm, at which point the Brown family purchased the property. In 1825, the Goodfellow family received title to the property from the Commonwealth of Massachusetts by paying a small fee to the Commonwealth and, in addition, breaking the sod on the land, tilling the soil, residing on the property for a period of several continuous years, and growing crops on the land. The Commonwealth of Massachusetts gained title to the property when it was founded as a State in 1787. That is where the chain of title to Acme's property began. The chain of title can be traced back to 1787. The land obviously existed for hundreds and thousands of years prior to that. Who had title to that land prior to 1787? And how it was that in 1787 an entity called the Commonwealth of Massachusetts became the title owner under the property laws of the United States? Prior to 1787 one could not find anyone who actually laid claim to that land in the modern sense of ownership. The land was wilderness—used and inhabited largely by the tribes of Iroquois Indians who were predominant in that part of what is now western Massachusetts. The Iroquois and other neighboring tribes moved freely throughout the New England area in the 1700s and for several hundred years prior to that, hunting and farming, and from time to time moving the locations of their villages.

Looking back to determine how this first link in the chain of title came to be, one has to continue to walk backward in time to see what happened in what is now western Massachusetts. In the 1600s, people sailed from England and settled on the eastern coast of the United States; the eastern side of what became Massachusetts. The King of England, from his vantage point across the Atlantic, granted ownership of property in the colonies. In most cases the King of England, and kings of other conquering European nations, laid claim to and subsequently granted ownership to vast swaths of land to either: 1) large mercantile companies to encourage them to bring natural resources back to the home country or, 2) wealthy aristocrats to reward them for loyalty and service to the monarchy. Their right to claim and dispose of land in this manner flowed largely from the divine right of kings, the theory that their virtually unlimited powers were bestowed upon them by God. When the Revolutionary War broke out, the title to the Colony of Massachusetts was transferred to a new government called the Commonwealth of Massachusetts. Vast tracts of land that had not been transferred by that time to someone else became the property of the Commonwealth of Massachusetts. So while Acme's chain of title to its property in western Massachusetts could be traced back in court records to 1778, actually it traces back to the 1600s when the King of England laid claim to ownership of all of the land encompassed by what is now the State of Massachusetts.

From the late 1600s on into the 1800s, there were a series of wars fought between the indigenous Native American tribes who had inhabited that land for hundreds of years and the various governmental entities that were laying claim to it—from the British monarchy to the United States government. The Native Americans all the while claim that they had used and had access to the land for generations for hunting and trapping and providing a way of life to them.

With some not terribly significant differences, this is the process that has taken place with respect to virtually every piece of real property located anywhere in the United States and, for that matter, in virtually every part of the world today. The chain of title followed a somewhat similar path where a government or a monarch laid claim to a vast territory of land and then began distributing ownership to that land in large and small pieces as it saw fit for a variety of reasons, some economic, some the result of political favors being distributed.

This same process continues. In the past 2,000 years, it has not changed. In the arctic regions of the globe, there are a number of countries including the United States, Canada, Russia, Greenland, Iceland, and some of the Scandinavian countries laying claim to vast areas in the arctic through the highly refined legal and diplomatic process of planting a flag and claiming it as their territory. And while there has been a treaty in place for decades covering Antarctica, no similar treaty has ever been negotiated or signed among nations to cover the Arctic (Struzik, 2010).

The driver behind this process is economics. Countries are vying for the mineral rights to anything that lies under the arctic regions and shipping lanes that are now starting to open year-round due to global warming. In many respects, nothing has changed from the 1400s and 1500s to the current time. Countries just embark on ventures to new parts of the globe, pound their flag into the ground, and say that this land is now owned by Country A, B, or C. If the past is any guide, which it undoubtedly will be, parcels of this newly claimed territory will be sold off by the claiming governments to corporations, which will then develop them as they see fit under some very loose guidelines set out by the claiming country. The land, or ice-covered sea in this instance, will be sold for oil exploration, fishing rights, anything that may have economic value. That wild, uninhabited part of the globe will be deemed owned by various governments and therefore be able to be sold to private entities for economic exploitation. Similarly, vast areas of the Pacific Ocean called the South China Sea are now being claimed as the property of a number of nations (China, Vietnam, Laos) because of their productive fishing beds, potential oil fields lying beneath, and advantageous shipping lanes.

The legitimacy of these initial links in the chain of title to property all over the world must be questioned from two standpoints. The first question is this: operating at some unique point in the timeline of history, on what authority (legal and/or moral) did a government or a monarch have the right to grant ownership to any piece of land in perpetuity? Was it a transient government that may have existed for a brief period in history but no longer exists today? Examples of this abound in ancient Europe; the Ottoman Empire, the Hapsburg Monarchy, and contemporary examples like Czechoslovakia. So did grants of right and title to land made under circumstances fleetingly in existence in the 1300s, 1500s, or even recently, dictate who will have title to that land for eternity?

The second question that must be asked is: what was the legitimacy of the government or monarchy when it granted title to parcels of land it claimed to own? Most of the monarchies that dominated the settled parts of the world from the tenth through the eighteenth centuries were families who had risen to power by the force of arms and the conferral of alleged divine right by popes. The concepts of democracy under which, arguably, the people inhabiting the land have, or should have had some level of input in, or control over, the decisions made about the land, did not start to form until the eighteenth century.

We have not moved far beyond the monarchy-controlled world of mediaeval times. One need only look around the world. The majority of the globe is controlled by governments ranging from totalitarian dictatorships pretending to be legitimate governments (Russia and China, for instance) to governments controlled by demonic, despotic, psychopaths (many African nations, much of the Arab world, Venezuela, North Korea, and on and on) to "legitimate" democracies such as the United States, India, and much of Western Europe. For hundreds of years, as civilization has moved round the world, the world itself has been cut up, subdivided, and parceled out to individuals and entities... and under whose authority?

The grantors range from legitimate governments that may have existed for a relatively long period such as the United States (1789), Switzerland (1848), and New Zealand (1857), to governments that may have had historical legitimacy but did not exist for very long (Moldavia, Republic of Vietnam, Ukrainian People's Republic), to brazenly illegitimate, despotic dictatorships (Libya, Saudi Arabia, Syria, North Korea, Sudan, Chad, Niger, Angola, Yemen).

Even under current notions of private property, and title to private property, the questions of the legitimacy of the grantors are profound. There is nothing organic or preordained about the set of laws that govern private property rights in the United States, or any country. Property laws are as fabricated and arbitrary as tax laws. Title to land has been developed to facilitate a specific economic order. The underlying principles of private property that operate in the US are by no means the only possible set of rules that would allow the US society to function or the US economy to survive.

This leads to the question: Who does land legitimately belong to and who has true legitimate authority to exercise control over it, dictating how it is used and how ownership passes over time? It can be argued that no one person, or people, at one point in time have any legitimate right to lay claim to the land and make decisions that will forever change the composition, control, ownership, and uses to which that land is put for hundreds and hundreds of years. The arctic region of the globe is the modern-day example of arbitrarily carving up the land. The polar region of the earth is a foreboding part of the world that is much the way it has been for more than ten thousand years. It has been inhabited by a variety of animal and sea life, and an occasional Canadian or Alaskan indigenous tribe member who might wander into that area on a hunting or fishing expedition. No one until recent time has purported to lay claim to it as their sovereign territory. Until as recently as the nineteenth century, explorers were not even able to access that part of the globe.

Now due to changes in technology, and climate, a relatively large number of people from a variety of countries can access that part of the world. We now have a situation where a number of those sovereign entities are attempting to lay claim to that part of the world. It seems to be without any real moral justification, for example, that the United States, due to its technical prowess and rich coffers, can move into the arctic region, plant a flag, and say that it now owns large swaths of the arctic. A simple act of putting a flag into the polar ice, running laser lights across the land, and transferring those boundaries to a map, seems a shallow basis upon which to say that the United States will now dictate who will have clear title to vast tracts of that region.

Another glaring anomaly is found with current land ownership systems in Third World parts of the globe. Increasingly, foreign companies are going into developing countries for the purpose of extracting a variety of natural resources the exploitation of which will profit those companies immensely and also allow the governments of the country of domicile of those companies to prosper. The oil that is drilled from nations in Africa and Latin America and the Pacific region, the forests that are cut down in South America, Indonesia, and other Pacific countries, and the rare earth minerals that are extracted from African nations, are not being used in those host countries. The value of those resources is being extracted from the Third World countries and *exported* to developed nations, which have the wherewithal to use those resources to manufacture highly sophisticated products. There are very few cases in the world where the people in Third World countries have benefited significantly from the fact that those resources were extracted from their countries. What tends to happen in the case of resource exploitation is that foreign entities come into a relatively impoverished country; extract some very high-value natural resources, and in the process do significant environmental damage to the host country, leave little behind either physical or institutional infrastructure upon which the host country can build its economy, and leave a huge remediation tab with no one to pay it (Rinat, 2013). It would seem from a sense of justice and fairness that this kind of activity shines a bright light on the problem. This resource exploitation is all done under the rubric of land ownership; the government of the host country (often corrupt, often incompetent) "sells" the land or mineral rights to a company from another country.

The moral justification and legal justification of the US current system of land ownership is thus rightly questioned as we consider the governments that over time and around the world that have purported to grant ownership rights, but so is the economic justification. The economic justification is called into question as we consider the vastly different timelines of the land itself compared with the timeline of the landowner.

So what is an alternative to this? How do we reconcile the notion that one man, who will occupy any place on this earth for perhaps about eighty years, will, in that short span of time, have the ability to dictate how that piece of land will be used from that day forward in perpetuity (the issue of alienability)?[5] And if the US current notion of private property ownership does not weather attacks from an economic, moral, or legal perspective, who then owns the land? The tenure of any one person's lifetime or even a few generations of lifetimes put together is a mere blink of the eye compared to the timeline over which the land exists. A myriad of questions arise.

Going back to the example of the mountaintop coal mining that takes place in the Eastern part of the United States, or other extraction industries around the country, the presumed economic justification to an individual or a company (i.e., leveling the mountain to extract coal from it) precludes things that can't even be imagined on the horizon at this point in time. The loss of that mountain may mean the loss of species of plants, animals, or even other minerals that may in future generations have far more value

---

5. Cornell Law School, Legal Information Institute, Alienable.

than the coal for which the mountain is torn down in the present. We are seeing that minerals and metals that were not even known to exist forty and fifty years ago are becoming the drivers of the US economies in the twenty-first century. In an economic sense, we might be tearing down a mountain to get the low-hanging fruit, coal for example, not realizing that we may be destroying much more valuable and high-grade minerals.

Stewardship Versus Ownership

Given the fundamental flaws in the current US system of land ownership (legal, moral, and economic), a different form of care and control of land should be considered—stewardship. Land ownership carries with it a number of attributes. The landowner has the title or a fee that can be passed on to others by sale, gift, or inheritance. Ownership of land in the United States allows the owner the right to do with the land as he or she sees fit undisturbed by anyone; limited to some degree by local ordinances, laws, zoning restrictions, etc. This is the "right to quiet enjoyment" of the property.

Depending upon the location of the property there may be restrictions attached to it for residential or commercial use, and activities on the land may be restricted so that his use of the land does not become a nuisance to adjoining or nearby landowners. Restrictions that attach to land often can be and are changed, only requiring that the landowner go through certain procedural processes.

The primary difference between stewardship and ownership is the alienability of the land. There would be slightly greater restrictions on the use of the land under stewardship, but these will largely flow from the fact that the land steward knows that at some predetermined point in time the land will revert back to the commonweal. This reversion attribute would operate similarly to that in a lease of personal property. Most leases contain provisions that state that at the end of the lease the asset must be returned to the lessor in the same or better condition as when the lessee took possession. The lessee gets the exclusive use of the property and right to quiet enjoyment of the asset, but the lessee's thinking as he uses the property is that, at the end of the term (be it hours, days, months, or years), he must return it to the lessor/owner. At the end of the term, the steward cannot sell or bequeath the property to anyone. He does not have the fee with which to do that. Now that we have begun to define the concept of stewardship, we can detail its attributes.

The underlying notion of land stewardship would encompass the concepts of using the land well and wisely. Couple that with the idea that the land is going to exist for eons of time and will be passed on through dozens, hundreds, maybe thousands of generations. The person who is walking the land today has an obligation to use it wisely in the context of current times and to use it well in the sense that it must be largely preserved and not degraded to the point that future generations will not be able to also have the opportunity to benefit from that land.

Land has basically two purposes: economic and aesthetic. The rules controlling economic stewardship might be quite different from those that control aesthetic land stewardship. In an economic sense of course, land would be managed for economic gain or profit. The estate that the steward of the land would hold might look in some regard like what we would call a life estate in property, i.e. ownership interest in the land for the life of the individual titleholder. Under stewardship, the steward would also have control of the land, but for a finite period of time. S/he would not own the fee that he could then transfer from generation to generation but would hold that stewardship over the land for a certain period of years, possibly fifty or a hundred years. A piece of property held for economic stewardship might be the location of a manufacturing facility, factory, a mining operation. This would obviously require that the steward have control of that property for a long enough period to be able to economically invest whatever was required to profitably extract value from that land.

Since the concept of stewardship implies that the steward at some point, whether fifty or hundred years in the future, will hand that piece of land over to another person or entity, one of the overriding concepts is that he must not do anything to unreasonably diminish the economic or vital to humanity value of that property for future stewards of that land. Clearly a set of laws and regulations would need to be developed to control and guide what is unreasonable or excessive diminishment or endangerment of the land. Going back to a prior example, a coal mining company might be able to mine underground if it did so in an environmentally or ecologically sound manner so that the land was not destroyed for future generations. It might seem to clearly prohibit lobbing a top off a mountain, thereby completely precluding and forever destroying a number of uses to which that land might be put. Another controlling concept of economic stewardship of land would be that the steward would pay a just and remunerative amount of money to the owner of the land just as lessees now pay a fee, a lease rate, to the owner/lessor. The payment would presumably be made to the community in which the land is situated, and thus compensate the people of that community for the value that the steward is gaining from using their land, depleting a resource, extracting a mineral, whatever. The payment would need to be commensurate with the activity that the steward is profiting from, profiting from something he does not own.

Aesthetic land stewardship would be managed under an entirely different set of constraints and rules. The pieces of land whose predominant value rests in their sheer physical beauty, habitat for endangered species, critical role in ecosystems, such as mountain ranges, lakes, rivers, scenic meadows: things of that nature whose existence generally provides for peoples' recreation, enjoyment, health, and well-being would require a very different set of governing rules and laws. This type of land would need to be managed with an eye on preservation for all future generations and an eye on maximizing the recreational enjoyment of the land by the current and future generations.

Economic and Aesthetic Stewardship

As stated previously, uses to which land can be put can be divided into two categories. Land is used as an input in economic activity and production—farmland, mining land, a site for a factory. The necessary place that land occupies in these economic activities is clear. Even residential property arguably falls into this category. The land on which a house sits has a measurable economic value just as rental property does. The value of residential property is often analyzed in terms of its equivalent rental value. As a matter of fact, in the current economic paradigm, lease versus purchase analysis is often done with respect to housing. As a result of the bursting of the housing bubble in 2008, this type of analysis will likely become more prevalent. Real estate companies and investors frequently refer to what is the "highest and best use" of a piece of property. The notion of highest and best use would likely come into play as businesses bid against one another to take on stewardship of pieces of land and bid to use the land for five, ten, fifty, or more years. But at the end of the stewardship, the land reverts to the owner, the community.

The other use to which land can be put might be termed aesthetic. This is the land on which recreation takes place; people hike, camp; artists find inspiration in vistas; land that is set aside to protect endangered species; land needed to remain untouched to clean the air; etc. As we go through the day, our feet quite literally always touch the land. But if we are not on property where we are earning a livelihood, or someone is earning a livelihood, we are someplace where we are recreating, resting, enjoying free time. Virtually all uses of land fall into one of these two categories.

Once the uses for land have been defined, it is necessary to consider how best to separate the timeline of people who will inhabit and use the land from the timeline of the land itself. The timeline of the people upon the land is measured in terms of a generation: thirty years. The timeline for the land itself is for all intents and purposes endless. Herein lies the necessity to develop a concept for the use of land (is it economic or aesthetic) that takes into account the vastly different periods of time that the land will exist and the person controlling that land will exist. We will start with land that has economic value.

There is tremendous economic inefficiency created by the current concept of private property when viewed through the lens of the US current market, capitalistic system. This rises largely due to the difference in timelines between land itself and the time horizon of a person or entity purchasing (hence valuing) a piece of property. When a person buys an economic asset, his analysis of the value of that asset will be determined on its market price or on a projected net cash flow from the asset (Tracy, 2020). That cash flow will be determined by the life of the asset (the period over which it will generate the cash flow), a projection of how the cash flow might change over the asset's life as it might be altered or enhanced or improved with new technologies, and what the asset may be worth at the end of the analysis horizon (salvage value). This same type of analysis takes place with land. The distortion in valuation takes place because the party analyzing the land may look out ten, twenty, fifty years; the land will exist for ten, twenty, fifty millennia. The value that the land may take on over that timeframe is incapable of being captured today.

An example may help illustrate this. Take a 1,000-acre parcel of land in the Appalachian region of the United States or in the West. The land is purchased by ABC Coal Company which proceeds to operate an open pit mining operation on the land. ABC estimates that the coal on the land can be economically extracted over a period of thirty years. ABC buys the land based on the current and projected price of coal over the next thirty years; assuming that at the end of thirty years a nominal amount of remediation will need to be done on the land to comply with current regulations. After thirty years the land will have little economic value since its coal will be depleted and there will be a significant amount of semi toxic residue on the land resulting from the years of mining. In 1980, given the price of coal and the demand for fossil fuels, ABC made a reasonable business decision. Fast forward thirty years to 2010. The price of coal has dropped significantly as alternate sources of fuel have begun taking market share from coal: cheap natural gas, renewable wind, solar, etc. At the same time, the prices of a number of heavy metals have soared as they are critical ingredients in many of the new electronic devices found in cars, computers, all types of next generation manufacturing equipment. Traces of these heavy metals have been found on the 1,000-acre parcel mined by ABC but it was removed, for the most part, during the mining operation. If the 1,000-acre parcel were intact in 2010, its value would be far greater than what was paid for it in 1980. ABC, as it turns out, merely took the low-hanging fruit from the land. ABC made a decision based upon a thirty-year time horizon; ABC may not exist much longer than thirty years; the land, scarred as it is, will last for millennia.

In the United States, today, more real property is being acquired for aesthetic purposes than used to be the case in the early settling days of the United States. In the 1700s, in the 1800s, and the early part of the 1900s, land was essentially acquired by people so that they, in one way or another, could earn a livelihood or at least reap an economic profit from the land in some way, such as investing in and holding the land in the hope of increased value and a future profit. Over the last few decades more property is being acquired by people who want a quiet piece of land for the solitude, a vista of an ocean, a lake, a mountain, and to have a place to keep a hobby farm to raise some horses; a variety of activities that clearly are not of an economic nature but of an aesthetic nature. The notion of ownership of real property starts to raise some interesting questions. At the extreme economic scenario, does Massey Coal Company's right of ownership to a mountain range in West Virginia give them the right to go in and quite literally remove the top of a mountain that has been in existence for thousands of years so that they can extract coal from that and thereby sell the coal and profit from it. Theoretically it would be possible for a company like Rio Tinto to buy major portions of the State of West Virginia, level most of the Appalachian Mountains within the State to extract coal and other minerals and turn it into a piece of property that would look more like Kansas from aerial photos than the way it does today. Extreme situations, yes, but in smaller scales this can be done and is being done all over the United States and all over the world.

In the aesthetic sense, does the US concept of ownership give Ted Turner, or like-minded billionaires, the right to buy millions of acres of land in the Western part of the country that encompasses mountain ranges, lakes, streams, high plains, prairies, and then set all of that land off-limits to anyone but himself, his family members and a relatively small number of people that he might choose to ever again have the right to set foot on that land.[6] At the extreme you could envision a situation where a wealthy individual might buy most of the State of Montana and post no trespassing signs around the vast majority of it. The rest of the people of the United States would never again have the ability or the opportunity to walk on, see, camp on, vacation on the property.

The Economics of Land Ownership v. Stewardship

The current structure of land ownership opens the door wide for economic inefficiency and creates fertile ground for speculation. Approaching land in a very classical economic analysis, it is merely an input in a process. Again resorting to classical analysis of a manufacturing process, the necessary inputs are land, labor, and capital (in a broad sense, including buildings, machinery, working capital, etc.) Labor will have the shortest time horizon from a business standpoint. It is arguably the most sensitive to changes in pricing

6. *Love Money*, 2020.

as well. For example, if a company plans on setting up a manufacturing facility in a particular location, and a competing industry is bidding the wage rate up for welders in that locale, the new industry will have to pay the escalating wage rate for welders. Market forces impact labor rates very quickly.

Another way to look at this is that wage rates are extremely sensitive to supply-and-demand factors and the manufacturer, at least in the short term, must accept the market rates. The labor input walks in the door every morning at 8:00 a.m. and walks out the door every afternoon at 5:00 p.m. It gets repriced very quickly. Ownership of labor, in a sense, ends every day at quitting time. Examples of the volatile and sensitive labor market can be found throughout US history, the most recent example being the oil and gas industry, and most notably in North Dakota.

Capital is a more intermediate input in terms of time horizon. Machinery may have an economic life of three, five, or ten years, at which point it may either wear out or become economically obsolete. The factory itself may be built with a timeline of twenty, thirty, or more years in mind. But at the end of some more-or-less foreseeable time frame, every factory will become physically or technologically obsolete. At that point, the factory likely will be torn down or repurposed, i.e. ownership of it ends or changes hands and usage.

Land is quite different from both labor and capital. The time horizon for land is essentially endless. Once you purchase it, you own it forever. Therein lies the problem—the duration of ownership, hence control, of land. In standard present value analysis, we value something according to the stream of cash flows it will generate over time or what we estimate to be its future market value if ownership is motivated by investment and capital gain. Fundamental to present value theory is that cash flows received farther out in time have less value than cash flows earned in the near term. Regardless of the discount rate employed, cash flows received out twenty years and beyond are valued at close to zero. The buyer of a piece of land will pay a price based upon an implicit stream of cash flows that will come from that land whether it be farm land, a commercial construction site, or a tract of land for residential development. The market will price it in some way taking this into account.

Go back to the factory that might be built upon a particular parcel of land. At the end of the twenty or thirty-year time frame that the factory was projected to generate cash flows, the factory itself may well be worn out or depleted or obsolete. The land upon which it was built will remain intact for eons longer, if not degraded beyond usable levels. Another economic player will come forward thirty or forty years later and begin all over again to project a stream of cash flows from that land and assign a new value to the property. He may then offer to pay a negotiated amount to the original owner of the land. The original owner already extracted his value from the land, i.e. he received the stream of cash flows that he based his purchase price upon. Now he will extract a "windfall gain" (or loss); if he sells the land.

This scenario plays itself out continuously around urban areas all over the country and creates numerous legal and tax problems as it does so. Consider the family farm purchased from someone (a state, municipality, private company) who received the land as a grant a hundred or more years ago. The farmer paid a fair price at that time to grow crops on the land and sell his crops at a price he projected to make a fair return based upon the purchase price of the land. The land has long since been paid off. A hundred years later, his farm is now within earshot of a growing urban area. A local real estate company would like to buy his land to build a 200-home bedroom community to serve the growing urban area, or a manufacturing facility might like to purchase the land for a plant to manufacture drainage tile. The farmer (actually his descendants) has a very large windfall gain if he sells the land or he may face the common tax problem or eminent domain action. The new economic player's projected use of the land is now a "higher and better use," and the new property tax rate on the farm will reflect that. The cash flow from farming will no longer support the new tax rate, and the farm must be sold. In effect, the new economic player, or combination of players, has forced a sale of the land. On one hand the "forced" sale may seem an injustice to the family being forced to sell the farm, but on the other hand their gain on the sale may be extremely substantial. Much of that gain will in effect be a windfall to the farmer. His land will have increased in value, not because of the skill with which he farmed the land, but because of a completely exogenous factor—the urban area grew out to his farm. Had the land been situated amid good agricultural land it might have commanded a price of $5,000 to $10,000 per acre. Situated on the edge of an encroaching urban area, it might well sell for ten, twenty, or thirty times that much. A number of exogenous factors like this can significantly affect farm land such as this that are completely disconnected from anything the farmer did to his land. Climate change can make other competitive parts of the globe less productive, social and political unrest in foreign countries can impair agricultural output, newly imposed regulations can put formerly productive land off limits to farming, and so on.

Let us examine another scenario that plays out with land ownership; one that lends itself toward speculation and asset bubbles. Party A buys a 1,000-acre tract of land in 1950 with the intent of using it for a specific economic purpose (mineral extraction, logging, a manufacturing site). By 1990 Party A has completed his intended use of the land; his factory has either ceased manufacturing the product it was originally built to make, or the process may have been outsourced overseas to take advantage of cheaper labor markets. The land now sits idle. Party B has an economic use for the land and is willing to purchase the land for a "reasonable" price based upon the economic value to him of the property. Party A may not be willing to sell the land for anything that might be considered a fair market value because he thinks that the land may multiply in value over the next twenty or thirty years either as prime recreation property or the potential discovery of mineral deposits that are not even hinted at in the current time frame.

The land is essentially "locked away" from being recycled into its next productive economic use as Party A retains ownership for speculative purposes. This scenario has played out with paper companies that purchased huge tracts of land in the upper Midwest and the West and the panhandle of Florida, with railroads that were granted large tracts of land and kept large tracts of land locked away, and with mineral companies purchasing parcels of land that may harbor extractable resources. The ownership paradigm is this: land is often not put back into the stream of commerce and priced accordingly since, once paid for, there is often an incentive to hold the land for speculative purposes. The stewardship paradigm is: land is put back into the stream of commerce at periodic intervals (thirty, forty years) since it is essentially leased to a party for a finite term to use and return to the community.

The mechanism of economic land stewardship would not be hard to construct. We will assume that in all cases the landowner is the community where the land is situated; it may be the federal government, the state, a county, or a municipality. When a parcel of land comes up for bid, the potential "stewards" can bid the land for a term of stewardship that might run for three, five, fifty years. The owner could impose some restrictions like zoning restrictions commonly used. If an area is overly served with gas stations, the owner may not allow the parcel to be bid for and used for that purpose. If a parcel sits atop fragile groundwater resources, it may not be open to mining and drilling bids. Requiring land to be analyzed and paid for just like other inputs in any business (labor, utilities, transportation, raw materials) fits quite nicely into the US existing economic models. A business would determine the period of time over which it would operate, and it would price land accordingly, much like it determines how much it can expend on a physical plant and generate a positive return over a certain period of time.

If a company is outbid in the stewardship program, it merely means another business has a higher or better use for the parcel . . . just as if it were bidding for the purchase of the land. The end of the stewardship term is when the difference emerges. The land reverts to the owner, and the steward cannot "lock away" the property away for speculative purposes. If the business bid too aggressively initially to get the parcel, and his business model unraveled in ten years rather than twenty years, it could turn the parcel back and pay an early termination fee much like in a lease transaction. This would avoid bidders for a parcel bidding too much for a property, knowing full well that they could not productively utilize the land for the time frame they bid for.

Under stewardship, land would become a finite input into the business model just like every other input the business employs. Land no longer has an unquantifiable residual value that encourages speculation by those with the cash to buy it and hold it for decades.

Aesthetic Property

When someone steps off economic land, they by definition step onto aesthetic property. We camp on it, we hike across it, we sail on it; it is for many people the ultimate source of mental and spiritual rejuvenation. It is the place we go to relax, seek quiet, recharge our inner self. So why is it that often the best mountain vistas cannot be accessed, the most beautiful beaches cannot be walked on, some of the most serene and pristine wilderness areas cannot be enjoyed? The answer is private ownership of property.

As the concentration of wealth takes place at an increasing rate all over the globe, more and more large, beautiful tracts of land are being purchased to be enjoyed by those fortunate enough to be able to pay the price. This process is taking place at a rapid pace in the United States. Entire mountains have been gated off in Montana accessible only by the owners. Ted Turner has purchased about two million acres of land all over the western United States (Ortego, 2019). Larry Ellison, the cofounder of Oracle, has purchased Lanai, an entire island in Hawaii. More land, and more of the best land, is being purchased and the "no trespassing" sign is going up. Anyone who enjoys sport hunting and has walked miles of federal and state land has frequently experienced the "Private Property—Keep Out" greeting.

A Utilitarian Analysis of Aesthetic Land Ownership

Going back to the questions of the economic, moral, and legal underpinnings of the US land ownership system: is there an economic or moral or ethical basis to support the right of people to buy large and select pieces of land purely for their private enjoyment and recreational activities? Let's construct a simple model within which to think about this question: This hypothetical community consists of 1,000 acres and ten people. In this community, 100 acres are utilized as economic land as defined above. The employers, homes, and requisite retail establishments of the community of ten people fills up 100 acres. The remaining 900 acres are wooded with small ponds and streams running throughout. The income distribution of these ten people is such that nine people live at a middle-class level (whatever that may be for this particular community), and the remaining citizen has income and assets several hundred times greater than his nine fellow citizens. The one very wealthy individual purchases the 900 wooded acres (at this point it does not matter from whom he purchased the land), fences the entire area off, and enjoys the land as his own personal recreational estate.

One way to phrase the economic question: is the utility of the community maximized by having one person enjoy the 900 acres for recreation while the remaining nine people have no such land to use? The answer is clearly, no. Unless this community is so unique that the wealthy individual has unique characteristics and sensitivities that allow him to enjoy the solitude and tranquility of the

900 acre estate to a degree that dwarfs the ability of the other nine to appreciate the peace and relaxation found there, total utility is not maximized (a classic economic standard: the greatest utility for the greatest number of people). The wealthy individual's utility (happiness/enjoyment) would diminish less than the other nine individuals' utility would increase if the fence was taken down. In other words, the total utility of society would be enhanced by a larger increment if thousands of people could camp, fish, hike, and bike on Ted Turner's 2,000,000 acres, than Ted Turner's utility would be diminished by knowing from afar that people were using the land he once owned.

One final point to consider in the economic justification, or lack thereof, for private ownership of recreational land, I will call the "in perpetuity trap." Under current property law, once an individual acquires legal title to land by purchase, gift or devise, it is essentially theirs forever. The land is passed down to each succeeding generation under the estate laws. This has at times been referred to as controlling the land "from the grave." The original purchaser, now deceased, continues to dictate who will own the land. Going back to the model of the ten-person community, suppose the one wealthy individual, who we will assume purchased the 900 acres because he loved nature, the beauty of the land, and derived tremendous enjoyment/utility from being on that land, dies and leaves the estate to his one heir. The heir, it turns out, is an individual who hates the outdoors, anything resembling bucolic, hates bugs, fears animals, and generally likes to stay indoors. Now the utility being derived from the estate drops to zero. What began as a distribution of land that could not be justified in an economic sense can become, due to "in perpetuity" ownership, a case where no one derives any benefit from the land.

Having found no economic justification for private ownership of aesthetic property, examine the second leg of the three-legged stool: moral justification. Moral justification is a very subjective notion. The requirements to justify anything, in a moral sense, will vary depending up on a person's value system, religion, cultural background, educational experience, life experiences, etc. A notion that is very often used in this analysis is that of justice. Does justice imply equality of outcome or equality of opportunity? Rawls' views on justice, as discussed previously, provide one very sound way to apply notions of justice based generally upon concepts of equality of opportunity. Is there a moral justification that can be set forth to support the right of a small number of very wealthy people to acquire vast tracts of land solely for their personal recreational enjoyment?

Let us go back to the hypothetical community set out above. In this community, we have one person with total access to the recreational land and nine people with no access to the green space. Is it possible that only one person wants access to that land? Is it possible that only that one person has a nature that can enjoy that land, benefit mentally or spiritually from spending time in those wooded areas? The benefits to all people from having the ability to spend time in quiet, tranquil, beautiful places have been well documented. If justice is the metric we use to measure, or even find, moral justification, there is none. In this hypothetical community, the only way to find justice in the given land distribution requires us to believe that at some point in time all ten people started with equal resources (good family circumstances, good educations, similar mental and physical attributes) and over time only one person made good decisions, and nine did not.

Now bring this hypothetical community forward into the real world by adding nine zeros to the population. As the world population exceeds seven billion people, more people need to have more space in which to relax and re-energize. Cordoning off ever larger portions of a globe that is accommodating more and more people is moving in the wrong direction. Access to and availability of space needs to be fostered, not impaired.

The idea of moving blocks of private land back into the public domain is not revolutionary, extreme, or without precedent. Grand

Teton National park is widely held to be one of the most strikingly beautiful of all the national parks in the United States. It consists of over 300,000 acres of the most spectacular mountains, rivers, lakes, and meadows in North America. Over 2.5 million people enjoy the park each year. Yet until the 1920s most of the land that now makes up Grand Teton National Park was privately owned, and 2.5 million people annually were not able to enjoy that unique spot. In the 1920s, John D. Rockefeller began surreptitiously buying up much of the Jackson Hole Valley from the private landowners so that it could be donated to the National Park Service. Land that was once enjoyed by a few is now enjoyed by millions.

Aesthetic stewardship of land would probably look more like the land practices employed by state and national parks, where the land can be used and accessed relatively openly by all subject to, again, preservation constraints for future generations.

However, aesthetic stewardship would preclude someone from buying tracts of land and closing the gate forever on anyone ever being able to enjoy or walk the land. This would prevent the ultra-wealthy from buying an interest in vast swaths of land and allowing them to essentially put up the "no trespassing" signs on hundreds of thousands of acres and passing their "fee interest" in the land from generation to generation, thus controlling the land from the grave. As noted at the beginning of this chapter, Thomas Jefferson, considered one of the wisest men to build the institutions upon which the US was founded, questioned the idea of allowing real property to be passed from generation to generation.

Man, in any sense, is no more than a tenant on the land. We are here for a truly short period of time. The notion that we can, in that brief moment, stick a flag in the ground and say we own this land from here to eternity, almost seems nonsensical. If we continue to work within the current paradigm of ownership as we use it in the US economic and legal structures, then ownership would seem to reside in something much larger than an individual or a corporate entity. A notion of ownership would seem to have to reside almost in a flow of generations of people upon the land. For example, the land, if it belongs to anyone, would seem to belong to the people who inhabit that land from generation to generation. People come onto the land, live on the land, work on the land, and die on the land, and then it is occupied by the next generation, and the next, and the next. We are mere passers-by on land that has been and will be here for millenniums. We can no more "own" the land that we walk on by occupying it for a very short time than we can claim ownership to the patents on the automobile because we purchased a car at one time. At most, we can be wise and good stewards of the land.

CHAPTER 3

DEMAND

The Fulcrum of the US Economic system

"Capitalism is often defined as an economic system where private actors are allowed to own and control the use of property in accord with their own interests, and where the invisible hand of the pricing mechanism coordinates supply and demand in markets in a way that is automatically in the best interests of society."

—Bruce R. Scott, "The Political Economy of Capitalism.

What do we mean by demand? Is it what people want? Is it the things people wish they could have? Or does it refer to goods and services people need to get by minimally in life? Or is it nothing more than what people can afford to buy?

Arguably, the US economic system had its roots in the 1700s, which coincided with the onset of the Industrial Revolution. People began their long and relentless move from the farms to the cities in search of the jobs that were developing in what were becoming nascent urban areas. The advent of steam power and industrialization marked a major upheaval for how populations supported and organized themselves. The changes wrought in the eighteenth century have continued apace. The study and analysis of economic forces have also grown and developed dramatically over the last three hundred years. As people strove to explain the forces that were rapidly roiling society, new economic theories developed. Some lasted; some did not.

Markets for labor and capital were developing, and rules were being written that affected how those markets worked. Labor markets gave birth to guilds and eventually unions. Experimentation began with setting wage levels. Corporate structures were developed and refined. Sole proprietorship morphed into partnerships, which in turn evolved into corporations with limitations on personal liability. Capital markets developed and became more sophisticated. Funding mechanisms emerged initially with bank lending, then issuance of debt by the corporation, collateralized debt obligations, and more complicated ways to carve up debt and sell it to various funding groups. A natural extension was the development of markets to trade these instruments and write and trade options on them.

The laws regarding ownership of property have also undergone change. Change in the US economic system has taken place steadily for 300 years. In a sense, the way in which Americans have structured the economic aspects of the US society are a flash in the pan. People on Earth have been walking around feeding themselves and sheltering themselves for 6,000 years. For over 95 percent of the time that people have been wandering the globe taking care of themselves and others, or waging war on others, they have done it under very different rules.

As societies evolved, the means of and inputs into production progressed, the needs and desires of people took on new dimensions, populations grew and became more concentrated in their distribution. A constant in the structuring of economic orders has been that man has created ways to allocate finite and, in many cases, scarce resources among people living at the time. Whether working under a feudal system in the Middle Ages, a mercantile order in the sixteenth and seventeenth centuries (LaHaye), a socialistic model in the late nineteenth and early twentieth centuries, or a capitalistic free-enterprise system of some stripe, the underlying task of economic systems has been to allocate everything that exists. Who owns assets, natural and manmade? Who gets beneficial access to everything that is produced or has been produced? This is what economic systems do, and herein lies the most elemental components of economic systems: supply and demand.

Virtually every part of the US economic system, every law, rule, regulation, custom, and practice is connected directly to the concepts of supply and demand. Capital markets and the instruments they have spawned, labor markets and the rules they function under, much of the US legal framework (contract law, property law, intellectual property rights, tax law, etc.) all have footprints back to supply and demand. Economic systems of all structures control supply (what gets produced and how) and demand (who acquires what is produced and how).

Hundreds of years ago, feudal communities produced food and rudimentary consumer goods of which the workers received some portion, with the rest going to the landlords. In return, workers received protection from neighboring hostile tribes for themselves and their families (Cartwright, 2018, & LaHaye "Mercantilism"). Indigenous people in many countries had a much more communal approach to production and distribution. Everyone provided labor, hunting, and harvesting, and in return everyone was fed and clothed.

The mechanisms governing the balance between supply and demand have changed over the past several hundred years. How do we understand the idea of demand in the current US economy? The term *demand* flows constantly and fluidly through the US economic discourse, but how often do we reflect on everything that the term encompasses?

Since supply and demand are foundational concepts of the US economic system, we need a clear understanding of how to think about these terms, particularly demand. Before getting into more traditional economic discussion about demand, we will begin peeling the onion by thinking about demand in a more individual, common-sense manner: demand from the perspective of an individual as opposed to aggregate demand. Considering demand from a single person's vantage point or a family's vantage point makes sense, because aggregate demand, which we talk about in terms of the entire economy, is nothing more than the aggregation of everyone's individual preferences and choices as to how they will spend their money. So just how does "demand" fit into the US economic system, US markets? What is demand? Does demand define those goods and services we want? Does it refer to things we need at a bare minimum to survive? Or does demand define those things we can afford to buy? How does demand get registered in the US economy? How do we come to learn what people's demands are? How is the market informed of peoples' demands? And once peoples' demands have been identified, how does the market go about meeting them? Given that we live in a world of scarcity, whose demands get met?

The US economic system, every one that came before it and everyone that will come after, has one primary function: to allocate scarce resources among people; hence, find a balance between supply and demand. Whether we consider demand as those things we would like to have, those things we need to live a reasonably comfortable life, or those things we need for basic survival, they all define "demand" in one way or another.

We start looking for answers to these questions by looking at the demand for housing. Everyone needs to have place to live whether owned or rented; everyone needs a roof over their head. Hence, everyone has a demand for housing. Consider two households: one household has two bread winners, both attorneys, earning a combined salary of $400,000 per year. The other household also has two bread winners, both working at minimum wage jobs, with a combined income of $29,000 per year. The demand for housing for the attorneys is quite different from the demand for hosing of the minimum wage earners. The family with $400,000 of income might reasonably look for housing costing in excess of $1,000,000. With $400,000 of income, $280,000 after tax disposable income, and spending 30 percent of that income on housing (a rule of thumb in the housing market), the family could spend $7,000/month on housing. That amount would easily support the mortgage payment of $5,000 to $6,000 on a $1,000,000 home. On the other hand, the family working two minimum wage jobs would have approximately $725 per month to spend on housing, assuming they also spend 30 percent of their disposable income on housing (given their income level they will likely keep all of their gross income). That payment might possibly support the mortgage payment on a $125,000 house depending upon the cost of taxes and insurance. In reality, that income level will likely not support a home purchase, but will go to pay rent. The point is that while both households have a "demand" for housing, the product that each is looking for is vastly different other than to fall under the broad category of "housing." The $125,000 house will provide a place to live; so will a $1,000,000 house. But the $1,000,000 house will provide much more than warm, dry, safe housing.

Now let's consider a family of four living at various income levels experienced by many people: at the current poverty level ($24,000/year), with a single wage earner making the federal minimum wage ($14,500/year), with two wage earners making the federal minimum wage ($29,000), a family living at twice the federal poverty level ($48,000). No matter which way we slice income levels, all of the above strata reflect low to very modest income levels. Why are these characterizations of income important? Because at the end of 2018 the median income in the United States was just over $63,000. (US Census, 2020). Half of the income earners in the United States made less than $63,000. Almost half of the wage earners in the country fell into one of the various categories described above. The "demand" for housing for a family earning $30,000 to $60,000 is quite different than the dynamics of that demand for a family earning over $400,000.

Which family gets their demand for housing met, the attorneys or the family of minimum wage earners? Besides the character of the demand for housing being quite different for these two families, there is another major difference in their demand for housing. In classical economic analysis, the demand for housing at low-income levels is far more "inelastic" than at the upper levels. This means that over relevant changes of the price range for low-cost housing, the demand for housing by low-income people does not change much. If rent for a one-bedroom apartment in a city goes from $800/month to $960/month (20 percent increase) few people will fall out of that pool of renters. People looking for housing at low-income levels need housing. They need safe and affordable housing, of which there is a pronounced lack in the US.

If the price of million-dollar homes suddenly increases in a community to $1.2 million (20 percent increase) the number of home buyers looking at that stock of housing will likely see a measurable decline. With a dearth of affordable houses in the $50,000 income level price range (approximately $150,000) whether those prices move up 10 or 20 percent ($165,000 to $180,000), the demand remains relatively constant.

If rent on an apartment in a low-rent neighborhood goes from $750/month to $900/month, it will not necessarily cause people to vacate those apartments if there is not alternative low-rent housing to move to. A functional understanding of "demand," how it is defined and how it is measured, requires a clear differentiation of commodities and the quality and price ranges within commodities.

What type of housing was being built in the US in 2020? In January of 2020, the median price of new single-family homes was $328,000. (US Census & US Dept HUD). An often quoted rule of thumb is that a person (or household) should not spend more than one-third of their income on housing. In 2017 approximately 12 percent of the US population lived at or below the poverty line (Center for Poverty & Inequality (September 2020). For a family of four, the poverty level was $24,860 of income per year in 2017. The house payment on the median home built in 2019, assuming a thirty-year mortgage, 5 percent interest rate, principal and interest excluding taxes and insurance, financing 100 percent of the purchase price, would have been $1,450/month. The annual house payment, far short of the total cost of the house (principal, interest plus taxes, insurance, maintenance) would exceed $17,000. That would be approximately 70 percent of the annual income of a family of four living at the poverty level, not a sustainable payment.

Working backward through the calculation, a family of four living at the poverty level, spending one-third of their income on housing could afford a house worth about $120,000. This number is inflated because it does not take into account taxes, insurance, and maintenance. Taking these factors into account reduces the value of a house affordable to someone at the poverty level closer to $100,000. As happens often in economics, to find answers and relationships, critical assumptions are made that can call everything in the model into question. The ability of the low-income family of four to afford the $100,000 house rests upon two significant underlying assumptions: first, that there is an adequate supply of $100,000 houses (remember the median price of a new house in 2019 was almost three times that amount) and second, we assume this family could qualify for the mortgage, an extremely unlikely reality particularly following changes made to the banking laws after the 2007 recession.

The situation in the rental market is similar. Almost 50 percent of renters in most metropolitan areas are considered "burdened," meaning they spend over 35 percent of their income on rent (Salviati, 2019).

We will use "transportation" as another "product" for analytical purposes to reflect further on the concept of demand. The demand for transportation is a derived demand. The demand for movement is not something desired for itself, excepting possibly the Sunday afternoon joy ride that people had considered a form of entertainment in the 1950s and 1960s. Transportation is needed to get from point A to point B to accomplish some purpose; hence the demand is derived from the demand to get from A to B for some reason.

One of the most ubiquitous needs for transportation is to get to work. If the price of transportation goes up will people "demand" less transportation to get to work? Generally, no. If a person's means of getting to work is to drive a late-model SUV, and the price of a new SUV goes up over five years from $50,000 to $60,000, then when it comes time to replace the SUV, some number of consumers will not buy the new, more expensive SUV. The demand for high-end SUVs will drop somewhat in response to the increased price of the vehicles. The SUV buyer may buy a stripped-down version of the vehicle, purchase a sedan rather than an SUV, but will probably not forgo owning a car, since the prices on SUVs have risen by $10,000.

Middle and upper middle-class people will respond to changes in the pricing of new cars, and by extension the resulting changes in used-car prices, by moving down the demand curve, i.e. changing their preferences for cars over the broad range of available vehicles. Demand for transportation has an entirely different character for upper-income people than it does for lower-income people.

What does the demand of transportation mean for a person who falls into one of the lower-income definitions? Transportation has an importance of hierarchy for everyone, low-income people included. Everyone needs to get to their job. Everyone needs to be able to get to the grocery store, occasionally shop for clothes and other necessities. Upper-income people have a wide array of choices as to the quality of their "ride" in meeting their transportation demands and can adjust those choices in response to price changes.

The demand curves representative of the transportation needs of lower-income people are significantly different from those of more-affluent people. The supply-and-demand curves depicting the market for transportation of low-income people will be curves representative of prices for ten, twelve, fourteen-year-old automobiles and the price of public transportation.

The price of steel might go up, in turn raising the price of new cars, with a resulting change in the demand for new cars. The price of steel could double, and the impact on the prices of ten-year-old cars will be relatively minor. The price of oil could rise by 50 percent thus raising the price of gas at the pump commensurately. Such price changes would be expected to have a direct impact on the demand for expensive fuel-inefficient SUVs. In fact, this did happen in 2008 as gas prices spiked upward (Squatriglia, 2008). Changes in factors affecting the prices of automobiles, particularly high-end automobiles, would be expected to be reflected in shifts in the demand curve for transportation for middle- and upper-income individuals.

Even if rising gas prices caused an increase in the cost of public transportation, a bus ride, from $3 per ride (not uncommon in major metropolitan areas) to $3.50 per ride, a significant 17 percent increase, the demand among low-income people for that ride will likely be unchanged. In economic terms, the demand for public transportation among low-income people is very price inelastic over most relevant price ranges. The demand curves for public transportation and ten-year-old cars will be highly vertical over wide price ranges for low-income people, as they still need to get to work, and there are few if any lower-cost alternatives available to them.

In some major metropolitan areas in the US, it is quite possible to rely on mass transit. But the majority of people do not live in areas where mass transit is a viable transportation alternative. Even in most large cities, it can be necessary to take inordinate amounts of time, and transfer one or more times from one bus line to another to get to work. This leaves most Americans dependent upon the automobile to a great extent for transportation.

How affordable is an auto for lower-income people in the US?

The average price of a new car in 2019 was almost $37,000, which was heavily weighted by the large percentage of trucks and SUVs purchased new in 2019 (Bowman, 2019). The average price of a used sedan sold in 2019 was just over $20,000. The monthly payment on that car if financed over five years at 5 percent will be $377/month; approximately $4,500/year. This is well outside of the affordability figure of 10 percent of income (another a rule of thumb often quoted) that a family should spend on a car when relying on $22,000 or less income per year. Remember 15 percent of households make less than the poverty level. A basic new compact car cost over $20,000 in 2019, again beyond the ability of the very low-income to afford.

So whose demands does the market fulfill? Does the $400,000-income household get their million-dollar home? Do the minimum wage earners get their $900/month apartment? Does the SUV-buyer have adequate choices among which to pick a vehicle? Does the low-income person have sufficient options for a cheap, dependable car or sufficiently diverse bus routes to get to work and the grocery store? A more classical economic approach to these questions will shed additional light upon what we see anecdotally and know intuitively.

A large body of economic study has been built upon finding mechanisms that explain the relationships between supply and demand. Much of the early study of economics in the eighteenth, nineteenth, and twentieth centuries looked for those mechanisms that explain the equilibrium between supply and demand. The relationship between the two has been described in terms of relative prices between goods, the price and value added of labor, the price and value added of capital, marginal utility theory. Alfred Marshall, the nineteenth century economist whose work did much to develop the theory of supply-and-demand curves, based his theories largely upon changes in prices. Marshall's proposition (Blaug, 1996) relating prices of one good to another was depicted as:

$$\frac{MU_x}{P_x} = \frac{MU_y}{P_y}$$

Basically, this equality says that the marginal utility of commodity x (MU_x) relative to the marginal utility of commodity y (MU_y) for an individual depended upon the relative prices of x and y. Hence the utility that an individual finds in a particular good, a notion about the value one perceives in a good or service, is a function of the relative prices of the goods. The lower the price of x relative to the price of y, the more x a person will demand. Marshall's work resulted in developing the supply-and-demand curves found in all economics text books.

When these models were constructed in the eighteenth century, the universe of commodities that could be supplied was minuscule compared to all the goods and services that are supplied or can be purchased in the twenty-first century. Similarly, three hundred years ago, the basket of goods that anyone could even conceive of wanting or needing was extremely limited. While the basic concepts still hold, the vast differentiation that has taken place between the economic actors who respond to changes in the shape and movement of these supply-and-demand curves has changed how this graphic analysis of economic systems should be employed.

In a broad sense, if the cost of housing goes up, prices move from P_1 to P_2, the amount of housing demanded will decrease from Q_1 to Q_2. In time, this will cause a shift in the supply curve with a lowered supply of housing offered in response to the drop in demand. The increase in the price of housing could have resulted from a number of factors: an increase in the cost of lumber, an increase in the wage rate paid to carpenters and electricians, newly restrictive zoning ordinances that drive up the price of land for development, etc. In a general sense, this is all true and accurately depicts the interplay between supply and demand.

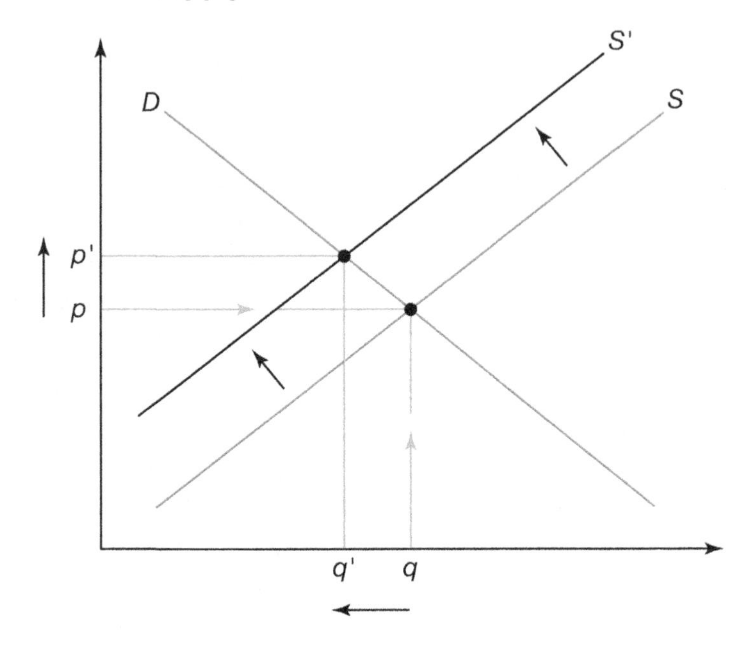

Figure 9. Changes in Demand Due to Changes in Price. *Source: 2013 Encyclopaedia Britannica, Inc*

Let's be more specific about the movement of these supply-and-demand curves. Assume several of the changes in the market take place resulting in an increase of 20 percent in building costs for housing. A house that prior to the cost increase would have cost $500,000 will now cost $600,000. The demand for that house will certainly drop. The cost of a 20 percent down payment has now increased by $20,000. The monthly payment on a thirty-year mortgage to finance that house has just increased by $500 to $600 per month. This is a house a family in the middle to upper-middle class earning close to $200,000 per year might reasonably expect to purchase. This family's demand for the $500,000 house, which has just increased to $600,000, will drop back to what, prior to the price escalation, had been a $400,000 house that is now increased to $480,000 due to the 20 percent price escalation.

This type of dynamic adjustment in demand is as the Figure 9 graphs depict. Over what relevant price range, i.e. income level, does the downward-sloping demand curve apply? For a family earning $200,000 or more, the demand curve in Figure 9 may fairly characterize their demand for housing. A slightly downward-sloping demand curve represents how they will react to changing prices for that commodity: a $500,000 house.

That tug of war between supply and demand has been described in a variety of ways. The common thread in most of these theories is the arbiter called price. This type of analysis makes sense in a closed system where all the participants in the system are economic actors. What does it take to participate in the US economic system? It takes money, cash in hand, or at least access to some form of credit.

Without money, the price elasticity of demand becomes a farcical concept. If the price of wool drops 50 percent with respect to the price of cotton, how much will the purchase of wool sweaters increase? If a person has no money, the answer of course is: it does not matter; s/he is not buying any new sweaters even if sheep start donating their wool for free.

Money is the required element to participate in the US economic system. Without money, demand cannot be registered, prices cannot be influenced. In a sense, dollars equal votes. Think about the implications this has for those with little or no money. Imagine a simple model with three individuals and two commodities.

Consumer A is in what we consider upper income in his society and has $1,000 cash in hand. Consumer B represents the middle class of his society and has $100 cash in hand. Consumer C is the prototype of the lowest economic strata with only $10 in cash.

The US marketplace has two products, X and Y. X represents consumer necessities such as food purchased at a grocery store, clothing, and housing. Commodity Y represents a basket of luxury goods: luxury vacations, food purchased at expensive restaurants, fine artwork. Further, assume that each unit of X costs $1 and each unit of Y costs $10. C lives very close to the poverty line and needs ten units of necessities to get through a year, i.e. he spends all his money on purchasing necessities. He could not buy one unit of Y even if he wanted to since that would leave him nothing left to purchase necessities for the year. B is better off. He can purchase the same amount of necessities as C, $10 worth, and still have $90 left over to purchase some luxury goods, Y. B could buy nine units of Y, but that would leave him with no money left over to save and/or invest. B would generally be expected to split his remaining $90 between a small portion of Y and leave some for savings, or a cushion in event of emergencies and other unforeseen expenses. This assumes that there are no differences of quality even to the necessities represented by X.

Economic actor B may choose to upgrade his purchases of necessities thus requiring more than $10 (while that is the case in the real world for illustrative purposes, it is assumed away). Individual A can purchase his necessities with $10 and be left with $990 to spend on everything else. He can buy ten units of Y and still have $890 left for savings and investment. He can buy fifty units of Y and still have $490 left for savings.

Viewing demand in the economy in this simplified way allows one to see some straightforward consequences of the demand side of the equation in the US economy. Assuming that suppliers respond to effective demand, a sweeping assumption that in realty has limitations, producers of goods and services that comprise the luxury goods bucket will respond to the price signs of individual A. To a much lesser extent they may respond to individual B. C has no impact on decisions made by producers of luxury goods.

On the other hand, all three individuals (A, B, and C) have an impact on the production decisions of goods deemed necessities: food, gasoline, basic clothing, haircuts, etc. As income and net worth decreases, the impact over a broad range of the production spectrum decreases. The ability to register demand is directly proportional to the amount of dollars/votes that an individual can bring to bear on the decision-making process.

Going back to the model, what happens to C if she gets laid off from her job? She can no longer even afford to purchase her basket of necessities labeled X. She no longer has the $10 needed to meet her annual needs for X/necessities. C has now fallen out of the market for all practical purposes. She not only continues to have needs for things—demand for food, shelter, clothing, medical care—but her needs will now differ dramatically from either A's or B's who remain as participants in the market. For example, C now needs to have very inexpensive housing available to her; think free shelter. Builders will not be lining up to innovate ways to build housing that is affordable to someone with few or no resources. At the same time, the construction of high-end housing will continue apace.

Production will always gravitate toward those products that have both the highest profit margins and the most stable group of consumers able to purchase them. In the domestic market, a number of government programs and numerous charitable organizations serve to fill demands, i.e. put money in someone's pocket by proxy, when the need arises. By and large however, people fall out of the system (out of the market) as their resources decrease.

Another way to frame the tension between supply and demand was set out by Jean Baptiste Say (1767–1832). Say was an early French economist who wrote a great deal about the issues of supply and demand. Say held that over time there was always an equilibrium between supply and demand; hence Say's Law $\Sigma P_1 D_1 = \Sigma P_1 S_1$ (Say, 1803). Essentially Say's law says that in the long run, aggregate demand will equal aggregate supply. If true, of course the implication is that the income earned by the producers of goods, both laborers and suppliers of capital, puts money into the hands of those suppliers of goods, both laborers and capital suppliers, which in turn creates demand—demand for consumer goods, demand for capital goods used by the private sector and the

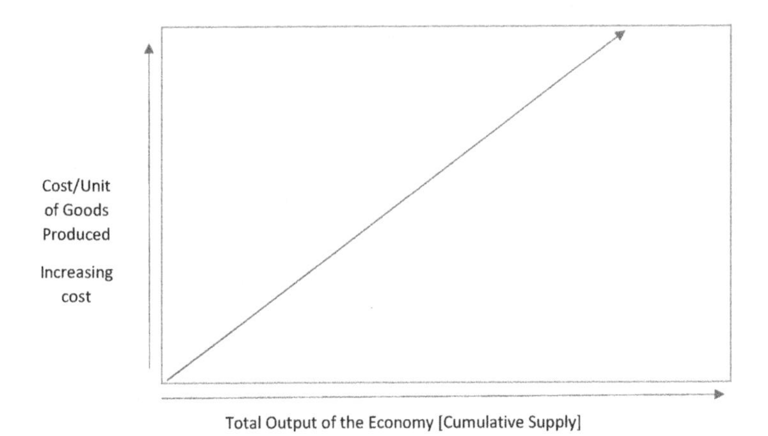

Figure 10. Cumulative Economic Output: cheapest to most-expensive commodities

public sector. This has a ring to it, much like the more current aphorism, "build it and they will come."

As producers make things, the production process generates income, which the recipients of that income then spend. In the aggregate, this is conceptually sound, and we could sit back and say that all is well and the system works. But does it? Does production create the means to buy what is produced?

The answer to that question requires further analysis. Income to the factors of production (labor and capital) does not flow seamlessly across to purchase what is produced, i.e. demand. Figure 10 depicts this issue.

The graph depicts the cumulative basket of goods and services produced by the economy, depicted on a scale of increasingly expensive goods produced. The US economy produces a staggering number of goods and services. Think about one common good, the automobile, specifically cars produced by Ford. The range of cost for Ford autos can start with the lowest-price Ford ranging from a $15,000 Ford Fiesta increasing to a $60,000 Ford Expedition. Cumulating the number of Fords at each price range (lowest to highest) would look like Figure 10, depicting cumulative value of all Fords produced. Now transfer this concept over all goods and services produced by the US economy. Essentially this is the "supply" side of the economy. Figure 10 can then depict the output (supply) of the economy cumulatively adding the least-expensive goods and services first as we move up the Y axis.

Now move to the other side of the economy—demand. Recall that under Say's analysis demand arises from the income paid to the factors of production, i.e. labor and capital. He posited that, over time and in aggregate, everything that is produced has a demand for it, and that demand is met because labor and capital earn income from their production activity in a sufficient amount to purchase everything that they produce. That economic law does not answer key relevant questions about the relationship between supply and demand. Who demands which goods and services as we move up the supply curve, looking at the curve as cumulating output from the least-expensive to the most-expensive as we move up the curve? Is demand, i.e. income, distributed evenly in such a manner that everyone can move up and down the supply scale with few limitations on the goods and services they can select and purchase?

If that is not the case, and we clearly know it is not, then how does that reality affect the distribution of goods and services that will be produced? Does supply beget demand as Say and Keynes might suggest? Or is it really the opposite—demand begets supply? This is not a distinction without a difference; this is at the heart of the US economic system.

Demand is measured in disposable income, spendable dollars. As pointed out, without money, there is no demand in the sense that we talk about it in the US economic system. Line A on figure 11 shows a situation where income is evenly distributed among the population. For example, following the line up, it shows that 60 percent of the population, measured on the X axis, receive 60 percent of national income, measured on the Y axis. Similarly, 80 percent of the people receive 80 percent of the national income. This straight line reflects total equality among people with respect

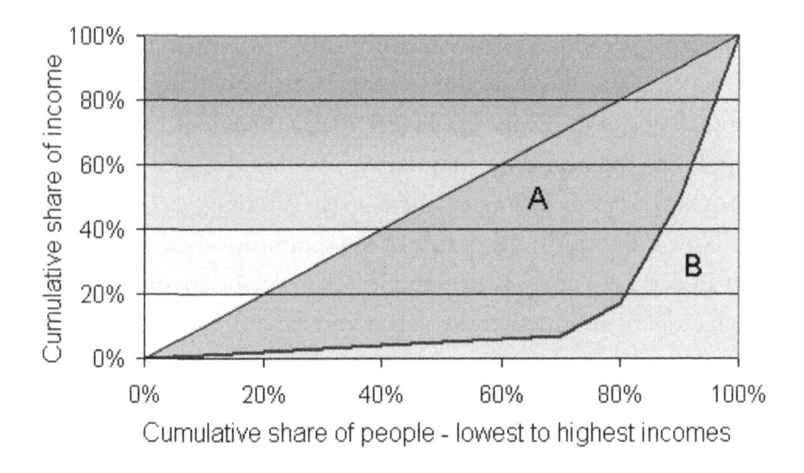

Figure 11. Cumulative Supply Mapped Against Cumulative Demand

to income received. This is the notion behind the Gini Coefficient, which measures the extent of inequality among people in terms of income received (US Census, 2016). This concept is discussed in greater detail in a following chapter. For now Figure11 is illustrative for the point.

Line B reflects more accurately the income distribution in the United States. The sharp upward slope of the curve as one moves from left to right indicates the rapidly increasing share of income that goes to a small percentage of the population. While this graph is for illustrative purposes only and not meant to reflect the actual income distribution in the United States, it is not too far off. In 2016 the Congressional Budget Office figures showed that the bottom 20 percent of the population received 4 percent of national income while the top 20 percent received approximately 40 percent of income (CBO, 2019). Letting line A depict the aggregate output of the economy (supply) and overlaying this with the aggregate income of the economy (demand) the issue becomes more clear. The lowest quintile (20 percent) of earners only have access to the lower components of the supply curve. Their income does not support purchases that fall further up the supply curve; those goods and services get costlier as we move up that curve. Similarly, higher-income groups (quintiles) can access greater and greater portions of the supply curve. However, it is not until one reaches the highest quintile of earners that the entire supply curve, the entire basket of goods and services produced can be accessed.

The graphical representation tells us what we all know in different ways. Those with the highest incomes can pick and choose among all the countless goods and services created by the economy. Producers respond to the signals sent by those with the most income. The demands of lower-income people get transmitted to smaller portions of the supply side of the economy. And as the graph depicts, when a person's income goes away, so too does their demand in an economic sense. Under these circumstances, a person falls out of the market completely, notwithstanding the fact that everyone needs to eat, sleep somewhere, get medical care, and be clothed, regardless of their circumstances.

The market is an unbiased mechanism when it comes to rationing of goods and services in society. The only color it sees is green. The system is set up to respond to demand that is registered in an objective manner: dollars register demand, and more dollars register more demand. Referring to the simple three-person model discussed above, if Consumer A purchases two or three new cars every two or three years, his voice is many decibels louder than consumer C who purchases one used car every eight or ten years.

Herein lies a fundamental problem with the US economic system. Demand will only be met to the extent one starts out or climbs to a fairly good level on the income ladder. When a person's resources disappear, whether for a few months, a few years, or a lifetime, that person effectively falls out of the economic system even though their demands do not go away.

How then does the market work for those individuals? If initial circumstances or the vagaries of life such as accident, health problems, or exogenous macroeconomic events like a pandemic turn against someone, the market's ability to continue to effectively to translate demand into services and products is abysmal.

What needs to be understood from this is that the feedback loop that is implicit in so much of the economic literature, the equilibrium between supply and demand, is not as simple as it seems. Many realities underlie this mechanism that need to be carefully examined, not the least of which is that it takes money and the ability to spend it, withhold it, and redirect it that provides the linkage to supply.

Much more thought needs to be given to how the uneven distribution of income and wealth impacts how efficiently the market works . . . even in traditional concepts of market efficiency. With the income and wealth disparities in the United States reaching one-hundred-year record proportions, the laboratory is in place to examine these questions.

CHAPTER 4

INFORMATION

Life Blood of Market Economies

You have a decision to make—an important one. In the short term, it will affect the health and development of your child. In the long term, it will have implications for the health and development of their children. The decision is a common one that most any parent has to confront: which baby formula to buy? It is easy to understand the immediate significance of this decision; it is up to parents to evaluate the available options and find the food with the highest nutrition, a taste that appeals to the fickle palette of a baby, and hopefully provide a child with what they will need to develop properly. To make this decision, information is needed. What is the nutritional content of the food? Does it contain ingredients that may be harmful to a child? What is important for proper development to begin with?

However, a facet of this decision is not immediate when the aisle is scanned. It is easy to forget that the shelves upon shelves of options were not put there by the hands of pediatricians, nutritionists, or child development experts—they were stocked by the invisible hand of market forces. Baby food choices made by parents in prior years provided information to baby food producers as to the consumer preferences for this product—that is, if more of one food is purchased than another, more of that food that sells well is produced. In this way, the choice confronting each parent has implications that will reach forward in time and quietly influence the very same decision when their own children must make it.

Once the stakes are clear, it is time to make a choice. In this case, product packaging is the primary source of information a producer provides on the details of the product in the immediate decision-making environment. Traditionally, this is where they educate consumers about their product. With television, internet, and social media, the reliance on packaging has diminished, but still holds tremendous sway in the decision-making process, as packaging is the most immediate impression a product provides.

The most important information needed to make this decision is the nutritional content and overall quality of the food; so this is what must be keyed into as the aisle is scanned. The first tub of baby formula often encountered has the following claims on the front label [brand name withheld]: No Artificial Growth Hormones*, Non-GMO**, Immune Support, Brain and Eye Development, Lutein-Vitamin E-DHA, and emphasized in the center: 2-FL HMO Human Milk Oligosaccharides*** (***not from human breast milk).

At first blush, this may seem like an impressive health resume. But even the least cynical of people are not filled with a sense of trust when reviewing these claims. S/he digs deeper.

The first * notes on the back of the package: "No significant difference has been shown between milk derived from rbST-treated cows and non-rbST-treated cows." Educated consumers may know that rBST is an artificial growth hormone called recombinant bovine somatotropin, which is given to cows to make them mature faster and produce more milk. But does this say whether rBST is bad for a child? To note it on the label seems to suggest so, but the statement makes no health claims either way, just a between-the-lines implication. The statement that a product has no artificial growth hormones actually means it *can* (is allowed to) have growth hormones, and in fact *can* be derived from cows treated with growth hormones, and (if it did) it has not been *shown* to increase those levels in this product. This claim seems a bit misleading.

According to the National Institutes of Health, milk from cows treated with rBST is as safe for human consumption as milk from untreated cows (NIH, 1990). But according to the American Cancer Society, the verdict is out on milk from rBST-treated cows. It is certainly bad for cows—increased instances of mastitis, lameness, and often requires that cows be given extra antibiotics to fight the higher occurrence of mastitis. Further complicating the issue is that it isn't rBST in milk per se that poses the potential threat, it's the higher levels of insulin-like growth factor (IGF-1) found in milk from these cows that is linked to increased chances of developing a number of cancers (American Cancer Society, 2014 & US FDA, 2020). As far as this label is concerned, this whole debate has been reduced to "No Artificial Growth Hormones"—a statement that isn't demonstrably false, but not fully honest. Meanwhile, the use of rBST in dairy cows is banned in Canada, the European Union, and some other countries.

The non-GMO claim's double asterisk is hidden so thoroughly that a microscope would be required to find it. "Immune Support" and "Brain and Eye Development" are not explained. Upon some quick standing-in-the-aisle googling it does appear however, that HMO (an important sugar found in human breast milk) does in fact increase several markers of immune system function (Goehring, 2016 & Good, et al. 2016).

Among the top sources listed in a cursory search of HMO is a trove of information found on the Nestle Nutrition Institute website, which happens to be owned by the parent company that makes this particular baby formula. All of these aspects of the formula are written in warm tones and bubbly fonts, up front on the packaging. The actual nutritional information on the back is in a very small, black-and-white table. This is just one option that must be evaluated and compared to the others next to it in order to accurately engage in the process that an Econ 101 textbook will say is necessary for the proper functioning of supply and demand. All the while, rows and rows of bright colors, happy cartoon babies, gold badges with authoritative-sounding certifications are written on jars, pouches, boxes, and tubs. A lot of information indeed when you have a fussy baby in tow that just needs to be fed and put to bed.

These are the two faces of the information dilemma in a market economy. That is, the information that consumers receive from producers about their products that allows them to evaluate the alternatives, and the information producers receive from consumers by way of their purchasing choices, thus communicating preferences and telling them what consumers would like to see more of on store shelves. This trading of information is the very constitutive ground of supply and demand. If an economy is to allocate scarce resources to the bundle of output that provides the greatest utility to the greatest number of people, this exchange of information must be as complete and accurate as possible. Without genuine meritocracy of goods and services, there is no genuine market economy.

The Role of Information in Supply and Demand

Let's go back for a minute and remember how the market functions, or how we want to think it functions. The market's primary function is to allocate scarce resources among people. Goods and services are produced in response to demand from consumers and businesses. The market then satisfies those demands. In that simplistic paradigm, the needs or desires of consumers (individuals, businesses, and/or governments) are conveyed to producers who then attempt to fill those wants in the most efficient, profitable manner. Demand is defined in economics as a function generally with six different arguments.

D_x = f (price, income, prices of related goods, tastes/preferences, expectations, and market size). The demand for good "x" is determined by those six factors, and how those factors affect that demand will vary from commodity to commodity. The factor to focus on in this discussion is preferences. What does the consumer want? How do those preferences get formed? And how do they get communicated to the supplier of whatever commodity we are talking about?

It would seem intuitive in the US economic model that information should flow largely from consumer to producer. As the general function for demand implies, several significant factors impact demand for any good, not the least of which is income. Herein we focus on the role information plays in that function.

The next line of inquiry seems to be: which way is most of the information flowing? Is it flowing from consumer to producer? Or is it the other way around? Ergo, does supply satisfy demand? Or does supply create demand? This is not a trivial question. It burrows down into the very core of the market system. If your view of the market is that it is a multifaceted system that allocates scarce resources to fulfill the needs and wants of people, then how information flows within that system is a fundamental element of what the system does or doesn't do.

What needs get met? Whose needs get met? If the US market system is not an organically evolved system but rather one that people have consciously constructed to work in certain ways and accomplish certain ends, then the question of whether supply begets demand or demand begets supply has important policy ramifications.

This leads back to fundamental questions about how information works in the economy. Does supply beget demand? Or does demand beget supply? How do consumers' demands get communicated to suppliers? How is information about what suppliers have created communicated to consumers?

Information might best be viewed as two distinct pipelines.

In one pipeline, consumers send information to suppliers, telling them what they need, want, and are willing to pay for. The other pipeline originates with suppliers and allows them to send information to consumers that describes the characteristics and details of what has been produced and offered to the consumer. How do these information flows work in the economy?

Information and the Trouble with the Rational Consumer

Take a closer look at these two pipelines, starting with the information consumers receive from producers. The economic principle underlying the idea of information as an organizing concept in a market economy has to do with the way people make decisions—what the US preferences are. The pertinent concept here is that of the "rational consumer." The rational consumer always chooses the alternative that maximizes their utility—the product that brings them the most satisfaction or that best meets their needs as they perceive them. This is the baby formula that will lead to the best outcome for your child. This theory posits the consumer essentially as a cost/benefit computer—taking in information about a product and its alternatives, weighing those based on the criteria that matter most to them, and choosing the one that leads to the greatest satisfaction of their needs. In this model, it can be seen how information is critical to the internal weighing of the alternatives.

This model requires two things: complete and full information, and a rational decision-making process. For all the tremendous powers of the human brain, this type of rational thinking is not a human strong suit. A better description would be that we are "rationalizing" creatures, far more than rational. The psychological underpinnings of how we make decisions and how we internally perceive our own decision-making process is tremendously complex and fills volumes of psychology texts. However, it is essential to understand the basics if we are to understand the role of information in the economy, because the companies responsible for informing consumers about their products understand it very well.

As humans, we essentially operate with two brains, two mutually dependent systems that coalesce in varying proportions to create one behavior—selecting one type of baby formula to purchase out of the myriad options. These two components of cognitive processing are called the automatic processes and controlled processes (Baumeister, et al., 2011). Ask yourself what is going through your head when you cross a busy street? Cars are coming from both directions at different speeds, crossing signals are about to change, you have to move at a certain pace to make it across a specific distance before cars are on top of you. People on the other side of the street are making the same calculations and indicating what their intentions are—it's a tremendous amount of information to have to process in a split second. When this happens, are you consciously evaluating all of this? Are you thinking out the problem in words and weighing your options? Give this a try next time you are in this situation; it is paralyzing. This is the domain of automatic processing. It speaks to us in feelings, in instantaneous emotional flashes of judgment (Bohner & Dickel, 2011). Enough space between cars, a sense of how fast you can move your body, and then from somewhere inside you, some feeling compels you to go for it or wait. The parts of the brain responsible for this are older, more primal. The automatic processes operate unnoticed, largely uncontrolled, and effortlessly; and they move fast; they have to. We are confronted with way too much stimuli in even the most routine of daily environments to consciously, deliberately evaluate them all—it is just too taxing and too slow.

The complement to the automatic processes is the controlled processes. If you have ever bought a car, you are likely acquainted with this component of cognitive processing. You may have deliberately compared gas mileage, thought about climate change and how the mpg may affect it. You considered payment options, you made deliberate forecasts about your budget and income—you did the math. In short, you labored over it. You had to deal with abstract things that were not in your immediate environment. This type of processing is intentionally initiated, deliberate, and more methodical (Barth, 1989). When you were working out your budget, were you internally deliberating about anything else? We have a limited capacity for this type of thinking—it is effortful and subsequently fatigable.

Now the problem. As much as we look inward and feel like a decision was deliberate and thought through rationally, it probably was not. We generally are not aware how much the decision was influenced by automatic processing that registered a flash of emotional judgment before the rational evaluation was added to our controlled processing queue. Think about the last time you were in a meeting and someone put doughnuts on the table. You see them and instantaneously your automatic processes register an emotional flash. Before you know it, you may be trying to talk yourself out of the feeling of desire. All the information you need is right there on the box, the calories per, the grams of fat—right there in a boring, small, black-and-white font. Right behind this though is a shiny, glazed, golden-brown doughnut that you can taste even before you take a bite. You look away, you reason with yourself about your weight-loss goals or think you will regret it should you pick up one. Next thing you know, you are taking your first bite. You will work out later—that lessens the sting—or maybe you walked up the stairs to get to the meeting. You did the hard thing and deserve it. That helps, right? What you experience in that moment is these two systems battling it out to create a singular action.

NYU psychologist Johnathan Height has described these two systems as being like an elephant and its rider (Height, 2006). The automatic processes are the elephant and are controlled by the rider. The reins are in our hands, and in certain situations we do have a measure of deliberate control. But if the elephant really wants a doughnut, we are just along for the ride.

This dynamic poses two problems for the proper functioning

of a market. First, alluded to above, is that of preferences. Was it your *preference* to eat the doughnut? You did it, so it could be argued that you did indeed prefer that alternative. But as anyone who has made a purchase, they knew in the moment they'd regret it later, that can be a pretty sloppy measure of someone's true preferences.

Research in advertising has shown that the emotional response a consumer has with respect to viewing an ad has a far-greater influence on their intent to buy that product than the actual content of the ad. This bias has been measured at 3 to 1 for television ads, and 2 to 1 for print media (Murray, 2013). As consumers, we are provided extraordinarily little actual information about good and services. Much more effort is spent on creating that initial, automatic, positive flash, because that is largely where our purchasing choices come from. What then are our actual *preferences* if our purchasing habits are so deliberately manipulated?

And the second problem has to do with the way these two systems process information. If the facts of the situation—the calories and fat in plain sight—didn't lead to a dispassionate weighing of the alternatives laid before you, can it really be said that the rational consumer as modeled in the textbooks truly exists?

Let's look at how this applies to an accurate and honest communication between producers and consumers.

On the supply side, the many facets of marketing and advertising are the conduit through which most product information is communicated. The large and growing investment in advertising in many industries attests to the fact that suppliers are working very hard and applying a lot of assets to see that the flow of information is going at a frenzied pace from the supplier to the consumer. Advertising budgets are increasing, and the advertising industry itself is growing exponentially with the help of the internet and social media. Facebook, one of the ten largest companies in the world based on market capitalization, is a powerful advertising/marketing platform. In April of 2018 when testifying before a Senate committee, Mark Zuckerberg famously (and sadly) informed Senator

Orin Hatch that Facebook made its money by selling advertising. Facebook's revenue stream grew from virtually nothing in 2007 to over $17 billion in the first quarter of 2020 (Facebook Investor Relations, 2020). Spending by the pharmaceutical industry on advertising increased from $17 billion in 1997 to over $30 billion annually in 2016 (The US is one of two countries in the world that allow the advertising of drugs to consumers).

The point is that suppliers are spending larger and larger amounts of money pushing their information to consumers, while there is no corollary of information being sent from consumers to producers. Would Humira and Lyrica have become household words but for massive amounts of advertising dollars spent on those drugs? (Ventola, 2011).

Query: would consumers be treated just as effectively for inflammation and pain by their doctors in the absence of the advertising?

Going back to the baby food aisle, let's look at what information consumers are receiving from producers. In light of the dual processing system operant in any decision-making environment, we can view ads, labels, and most any marketing as containing two types of information. The first is information that is necessary to the controlled processing side of our decision-making process—facts about nutrition, cost, materials, and what form the detailed specs of a product—that is, the information needed to evaluate alternatives with any semblance of a meritocratic process. The other is those things that influence the automatic processing side of the equation—color schemes, pictures of happy people using a product, celebrity endorsements, fonts and the like, which all influence that immediate registering of an emotional flash. This type of information is generally not considered in discussions of supply and demand and consumer *choice*.

In the case of the baby formula, the colors used on the packaging are no coincidence. Colors are one of the most immediate ways to influence automatic processing. This is very deliberate and has been studied in detail by psychologists and marketers. The primary text on the formula tub is in navy blue. This color has been shown to illicit feelings of security, trust, integrity, and authority. The rest of the label uses yellow (energetic, warm, perky, joy), pink (healthy, feminine, sweet, compassion), and light green (freshness, healing, Earth). Further, the packaging includes a picture of an attractive mother smiling proudly at her happy daughter. Pictures of smiling, attractive people, especially babies, light up parts of the brain associated with joy and happiness—it is contagious and creates an automatic positive emotional association (Berg, et al., 2015).

We cannot help but be influenced by these many factors that are far outside of the realm of what provides useful fodder for rational thinking. We cannot help it, and advertisers know this. In fact, the World Health Organization issued a report in 2012 stating that they have found that the baby food industry uses the same tactics as those found in the marketing of cigarettes (Granheim, et al., 2017). Far more resources are expended by producers in attempts to induce us to buy their products than in educating us about them. For the proper functioning of markets, this presents a fundamental breakdown.

The vast and growing amount of money spent by producers on advertising might just offer a little hint that a lot of the "stuff" the US economy produces does not result from an awakening on the part of consumers, that all of a sudden they realized they "needed" a lot of heretofore unheard-of products. But this is a difficult statement to evaluate empirically. Did you genuinely want or need that exercise bike with video classes? Or were you sold an idea that made finally getting in shape seem easier? Do you really need that pickup truck to drive around a suburb? Or could it be that through conditioning they conjure images of manly, tough guys, and that fits nicely into your self-image?

The problem is that we cannot empirically measure someone's desire or feelings of satisfaction from purchasing any good or service in any standardizable and comparable way. This is a problem that the likes of Jeremy Bentham and John Stewart Mill wrestled with. The solution they conceived of was that although we cannot empirically measure someone's satisfaction (joy, pleasure, *utility*), we can see how they choose between alternatives. In economic parlance, the catch-all term for the myriad varieties of positive feelings, sense of joy or satisfaction, associated with a good or service is termed its *utility*. If a red shirt, blue shirt, and green shirt are placed in front of a person and she chooses the blue, it can be argued that she anticipated deriving the most utility from the blue shirt. We cannot measure how much, but we can know that it is more than what she would have received from the red or green shirt—why else choose this above the alternatives? When this choice gets placed in front of people at the societal scale, it can be argued that whichever shirt is chosen the most provides the most utility to society, and thus resources are allocated efficiently if they are allocated to producing more blue shirts. This is a simple model of an economy, and at a certain point blue-shirt saturation will begin to undermine their utility-maximizing potential, but it is the very foundation of what constitutes a theoretically efficient allocation of resources.

Through the aggregate of peoples' expression of what causes them the most utility—what they choose to purchase over other options—resources are directed toward producing those things and subsequently utility is maximized for the society as a whole. But what if the producers of red shirts hired an attractive celebrity to model them while blue and green shirts sat on plain mannequins? Now there is more for your automatic processes to register. And if the celebrity is chosen well, they will register a positive flash. This distortion of preference at the very ground floor of consumer choice reverberates through the whole structure of the economy.

Aggregate purchasing habits as a way of measuring how scarce resources should be utilized efficiently is akin to how physicists detect planets by measuring distortions in the orbits of nearby objects—a measurement by proxy.

Let's look at another way of measuring the aggregate utility of our purchases via a proxy variable. If the aggregate choosing of certain goods and services over the alternatives is the best way to determine how to maximize societal utility (use resources efficiently), then the aggregate choice to lock our purchases away where we cannot interact with them should prove the inverse point. That is, if we actively choose to distance ourselves from our purchases, couldn't it be argued that this represents a misallocation of resources? An expression of *disutility* we are deriving from our consumptive choices?

If so, there is perhaps no better measure of how much stuff we buy that later provides us no utility than to look at the expansion of self-storage in the US. As of 2020, self-storage has become a $39 billion per year industry (Harris, 2020). It is also nine times what was spent on malaria research in 2016 (IHME, 2019), almost three times what was spent on the free student lunch program in 2019 (USDA, 2020) six and a half times what we spend on the Special Supplemental Nutrition Program for Women, Infants, and Children that provides critical nutritional support to mothers and children (Center on Budget and Policy Priorities, 2017). The things we purchased but no longer want/need now occupy more than 2.3 billion square feet in America. That is more than 7 square feet per capita in the United States. It would be physically possible for every man, woman, and child in the US to stand—all at the same time—under the total canopy of self-storage roofing. That is 82.5 square miles of things that we could not fit in US houses, garages, and attics. Imagine the untold trillions of dollars' worth of economic output that is languishing in storage units. Worse yet, imagine what could have been done with those resources had they been allocated to medical supplies, educational materials, and infrastructure. Were these unmet demands or products that we were convinced we needed? These are things economics should be concerning itself with.

The flow of information that informs the consumer as to the options available to them, and all of the associated characteristics of those products, is very large, well-funded, and highly focused.

The focus of the information flow from producer to consumer is becoming more focused all the time with advances in social network platforms and advances in technological capabilities to seek out individuals with predetermined preferences. It is clearly in producers' best interests to continue down this path and allocate increasing amounts of resources to these efforts. There is no conceivable reason a consumer would honestly ask for something s/he did not actually want or think that s/he wants. Consumers generally have no incentive to play hide-the-ball with the goods and services they want access to.

The simple notion of the market is that goods and services are offered to the consumer, and the consumer makes rational decisions about what s/he will purchase based upon complete information about the quality and content of the products between which the consumer can choose (prices of related goods referred to in the demand function above). The point is: what producers can convince consumers they need is not at all the same thing as consumers expressing their needs and producers responding. When the script is flipped in this way, it can hardly be said that resources are being allocated to their most efficient, utility-maximizing potential. Once again, does demand beget supply or supply create demand? The incentive for deception is completely one-sided; there are incentives for producers to be less than honest, there are none for the consumer. This is not to say that all producers of goods and services are deceptive in their advertising and marketing practices, but it is problem that can put sand in the wheels of the underpinnings of a market system.

So why would a manufacturer resist telling his customer what ingredients are in a product? Why would a food processor not want consumers to know that their product has GMO ingredients? Why do milk producers resist telling people their cows were treated with artificial growth hormones? Why do meat producers resist telling shoppers that their herds are treated with large amounts of antibiotics in order that they can reach market weight in shorter periods of time? Why do financial institutions resist giving customers easy-to-understand information about the fees attached to many of the products they offer? Why did car manufacturers drag their feet on telling car buyers what the gasoline mileage was for the cars they sold? Why did tobacco companies refuse for decades to admit to smokers that their product had a high likelihood of either killing them or incapacitating them? Why did the tobacco companies hide the fact that their product was laced with chemicals that made them more addictive? The answer to all of these questions is: of course, it would hurt sales. If there were full disclosure about many products and services offered in the marketplace, buyers might make other choices.

This whole discussion of information and its essential role in a market system brings us back to the question that prompted it: does supply satisfy demand, or is it the other way around? This question cannot be answered simply. We cannot just add up the aggregate of purchases that people were manipulated into making and weigh that against the number that were organic. Even if such an endeavor were attempted, much of the time we are not clearly aware of what side of the divide our own purchases fall. But given the amount of money spent on crafting marketing campaigns that do very little to educate consumers about the products available to them, it is safe to say what goods and services are available to us does not simply follow an honest recognition of what people need or want. This manipulation of preferences—an essential component of what constitutes demand—has tremendous implications for an efficient allocation of resources. Put simply, the information problem constitutes a significant market failure.

Where the Rubber Meets the Road With (Mis) Information

Housing: It is common knowledge that there is a lack of "affordable" housing in the US, housing that can be purchased by the lower half of income earners. Reflect back on the Great Recession and what happened to the housing market during that period and the time leading up to it. From 1990 until 2005, home ownership increased in the US from about 64 to 69 percent (US Census Bureau, 2020). This did not happen because the fundamentals of the housing market changed. People were not making significantly more income, and the price of houses was not decreasing. Quite the opposite was happening. Home prices continued to rise very steadily during this period. Enter the financial industry. Home buyers were told they could afford more expensive houses, and more prospective home buyers were told they could now afford houses. This was a byproduct of financial alchemy: no-doc loans, no interest loans, no down payment loans. The information flowing from the financial industry to home buyers was false. Home ownership was in reality not within the reach of vastly more people. A one-way flow of bad information from the financial industry to home buyers led to a very deep recession beginning in 2007. Consumers fell prey to that bad information.

Transportation: Are auto makers quickly retreating from the manufacture of sedans and smaller inexpensive cars because there is just not much demand for $15,000 cars? Or is their focus being trained on the SUV and truck market ($40,000 to $60,000) due to the huge profit margins in these vehicles? (Carey, 2018) Which type of vehicle are their advertising dollars being focused on? Auto makers have the usual advertising platforms for their cars: television, internet, print journalism, etc. Consumers do not take out ads in newspapers or write TV commercials. In 2020 Ford stopped selling any sedans and focused exclusively on SUVs, pickups, and crossovers. Query: did consumers somehow get the message through to auto makers that they no longer wanted or needed smaller more affordable sedan models? (Muller, 2018)

Food: Do consumers want to eat an ever-growing diet of highly processed foods dependent in their production on huge amounts of herbicides, pesticides, and antibiotics? Or have food suppliers marketed this type of food to the consumer due to the economic advantages of producing food in this manner? Food companies are constantly creating new food products and aggressively marketing them to consumers. While there are just no similar mechanisms for consumers to tell cereal companies, meat producers, and other food producers what they want to see on the grocery store shelf, the ability of consumers to withhold dollars from products is more effective in the food industry than say the auto industry, due to the smaller per item cost of the product and far larger numbers of substitute products available. But these decisions, especially the relatively small decisions that we make without the same level of scrutiny as larger purchases, are especially subject to manipulation via marketing practices.

Healthcare: There is a problem with information flow within healthcare in the US, but it is not really accurate to say that the problem exists within the healthcare market. Healthcare in the US does not fit within any reasonable definition of a market. If this were truly a market, would consumers of this product be satisfied that suppliers have given them a healthcare system that ranks 37th in the world in overall health outcomes? Would consumers have told suppliers they expect a system that ranks thirty-three of thirty-six OECD countries in infant mortality, thirty of thirty-six for obesity, and twenty-eight out of thirty-six for life expectancy? (United Health Foundation, 2018)

Of course not. Consumers in this market operate in the dark. Prices of what healthcare consumers *buy* are almost impossible to know particularly prior to *purchasing* the healthcare. This is because the prices of healthcare products are largely determined in secret negotiations between suppliers such as hospitals, pharmaceutical companies, doctor practice groups, and the insurance companies that pay for the products they deliver to consumers.

For the most part, only after the service has been provided or the procedure been performed will the consumer even see what the payer has been charged. This problem is only with the pricing aspect of what the consumer is purchasing. There is a huge lack of transparency on the quality of the service or procedure itself when it comes to healthcare. Healthcare providers do not make readily available the quality of their doctors in any particular practice within their systems. Why would they? It might lead to fewer patients. The systemic problems of lack of information transparency within the healthcare system are well documented in a book by Dr. Marty Makary, *The Price We Pay: What Broke American Health Care—And How to Fix It.* (Bloomsbury Publishing, 2019). Has healthcare just become another margin-driven consumer industry with suppliers marketing high-margin services to a public open to being told where their true needs lie?

Thoughts

If the market is to function as a system that allocates scarce resources, or assumes to, then what those scarce resources are allocated to and how they are rationed is fundamental to the entire system. It is clear to see how those allocations might differ depending upon whether demand drives supply or vice versa. If on the one hand, consumers (individuals, corporations, governmental entities) dictate what they want, and producers work to supply those products and services, you would get one resulting basket of goods and services from the market.

On the other hand, if suppliers dictated what goods and services they are interested in producing and concurrently work to sell those products to consumers, you will end up with a very different make up in the basket of goods and services on the market. If the latter is essentially how the US economy operates, the life blood of that system is marketing and advertising. The invisible hand that balances supply and demand starts to look a little more visible.

So who determines what comes out the end of this complex black box mechanism we call the economy? What does the US economy produce? Back to the earlier question: does it produce things that consumers decided they really need? Or does it produce things that manufacturers determine they can successfully sell to people with a good profit margin attached? The reality is probably some combination of the two.

One way to even attempt to get at the answer would be to go through a catalog of all things provided in the US economy and analyze each one in order to try to determine whether demand or supply was the parent of each one—an ominous and hopeless task. Yet at some level, this question must be asked as it bears on governmental policy dealing with the economy and the steps we might take to alter aspects of the US system. The importance of the question is woven into US discourse: political, policymaking, philosophical, etc.

When we resort to notions like, "The market will determine the best answer," or "The market will solve the problem," who are we actually leaving in the driver's seat? Policymakers need to understand their role in leveling the playing field, arbitrating the mismatched flow of information between producers and consumers.

The concept of not fully disclosing all information about a product or service flies in the face of the theoretical underpinning of the free market. Without an honest and open disclosure of information about goods and services, the market system becomes nothing more than a highly contrived shell game that pits consumer against producer, with the producer often hiding the truth about what s/he is producing from the consumer.

One of the larger "truth in labeling" fights undertaken recently concerns the use of genetically modified organisms (GMOs) in food products. Experts have lined up on both sides of the GMO battle, extolling the truth of their scientific findings as to the negative impacts of GMO ingredients, or the lack of evidence in that regard. Science aside, many people have very strong feelings about GMO ingredients. Giving a nod to the inconclusiveness of the debate about the long-term impacts of GMO products, ask yourself: why not put them on the label and let the consumer decide whether s/he wants to buy them? Why not make full disclosure about what goes into a product and let the market work? The answer is that only a naïve notion of how the US market works would support such a process. The largest laggard in the GMO labeling issue is the United States. Many of the largest agro-industrial companies are in the US as are many of the large seed producers and agrochemical companies. Here is the list of countries around the world that mandate GMO food-labeling laws:

Australia
Austria
Belarus
Belgium
Bolivia
Bosnia/Herzegovina
Brazil
Bulgaria
Cameroon
China
Croatia
Cyprus
Czech Republic
Denmark
Ecuador
El Salvador
Estonia
Ethiopia
Finland
France
Germany
Greece
Hungary
Iceland
India
Indonesia
Ireland
Italy
Japan
Jordan
Kazakhstan
Kenya
Latvia
Lithuania
Luxembourg
Malaysia
Mali
Malta
Mauritius
Netherlands
New Zealand
Norway
Peru
Poland
Portugal
Romania
Russia
Saudi Arabia
Senegal
Slovakia
Slovenia
South Africa
South Korea
Spain
Sri Lanka
Sweden
Switzerland
Taiwan

Thailand	Ukraine	Vietnam
Tunisia	United Kingdom	
Turkey		

Even Russia, Saudi Arabia, and Kazakhstan require some GMO labeling. The parts of the globe not represented in the list are North America and Africa. It is no surprise that a country that is home to the largest beneficiaries of a lack of truthfulness in GMO labeling has greatest lack of transparency in GMO labeling.

There is a parallel legal concept to the truth-in-labeling fights taking place in the market. The 5th Amendment allows a defendant in a criminal proceeding to refuse to testify and possibly incriminate himself. The fact finder (the jury) is told not to infer that the defendant is hiding their guilt by not testifying. The jury, being made up of largely rational individuals, then immediately turns around and assumes the defendant is hiding something if s/he refuses to testify.

The reasonable inference to be drawn by a consumer whenever a producer balks at fully disclosing ingredients in a product should be that the producer is hiding something. Not only would that be a humanly rational inference to draw, but history would argue that is a factually true conclusion to draw. Consider these deceptive practices that were finally uncovered:

- The practice by banks of clearing larger items first to increase overdraft fees (Touryalai, 2012).
- Deceptive "Animal Care Certified" label claims made on egg cartons about inhumane treatment of hens (Barrionuevo, 2005).
- Tobacco industry practice of deliberate false advertising for decades, deceiving the public about the safety of smoking cigarettes (Winter, 2012).

- Companies like W.R. Grace that failed to disclose the dangers associated with their asbestos products (AP, 2011).
- Ford Motor Company's continued sale of the defectively designed Pinto for seven years after knowing of gas tank defects would cause hundreds of people to burn to death (Dowie, 1977).
- Hyper-aggressive marketing of OxyContin that led to a drug epidemic (VanZee, 2009).

There is no place in a free market system for anything but full and honest disclosure about a product or service being offered in the marketplace. When a company or entire industry mounts an attack on openness in labeling, everyone's antenna should go up, and the obvious question should be asked: What are they hiding?

Information is the fundamental grease that allows the wheels of the economy to turn. Its importance is paramount to the system Americans have created, the paradigm Americans operate within. We are witnessing an exponential growth in the role of information in the world and experiencing the havoc that can be wreaked, even in the US political system, by the dissemination of untruthful information. So when the answer to a large social issue is, "The market will solve it," an alarm should go off and questions raised. Who is going to be putting forth the solutions? Can they be relied on to offer honest information to be brought to bear on the problem? Do they have incentives to be anything less than completely honest and open with policies and information put on the table?

CHAPTER 5

EXTERNALITIES

A Major Flaw in the System

Recall that the US free-market capitalist system operates, or we like to think it operates, under the following paradigm. Producers manufacture products in the most efficient, low-cost manner and put them into the marketplace in competition with other companies producing similar products, all trying to entice purchasers to buy their product. In a truly competitive market, being the low-cost producer, or one of the lowest cost producers, is critical, product quality differentiation notwithstanding. One needs look no further than the oftentimes rancorous negotiations that take place between labor and management in countless industries to appreciate the importance to a company of keeping its input costs at a minimum. Producers in almost every sector of the economy are on a constant mission to improve production processes, cut labor and material costs, reduce transportation costs, put more robotics onto the shop floor, etc. In the international arena, a hue and cry goes up when one country thinks its industries have a competitive disadvantage to those same industries in another country that is "unfairly subsidizing" its domestic industries and sending products into the other party's market at prices/costs below the actual cost to produce the product.

Another way a producer can lower its cost structure differs from directly cutting the price of inputs into its production process. A producer can shift some of its costs to another party. A producer can take advantage of "externalities." Externalities are essentially those costs (or benefits) that go uncaptured in the economic accounting system. They are costs or benefits that spill over onto someone other than the party who pays to incur the cost or actually enjoys the benefit. My purpose here is not to undertake a discussion of the origin of the concept of externalities or review the large swaths of academic literature dealing with externalities. Bear in mind: the purpose here is to take a rather expansive look at the paradigm that is the US economic system, calling into question fundamental parts of it that are often overlooked when we think about how efficiently the system is accomplishing what we want it to. The existence of externalities, and their impact on the economy, are significant reasons the market often fails to accomplish all of the beneficial things we ascribe to it.

Externalities take many different shapes and characters. Externalities basically describe the shifting of costs and benefits. And they can flow both ways. Externalities can allow a company to shift its costs of production onto parties not directly involved in the production process. On the other hand, externalities also exist when one party receives benefits from an activity that they did not incur the cost to produce. For example, education produces externalities in that many people who do not pay to support the cost of educating young people, ranging from pre-kindergarten through college, receive spillover benefits from the education those students receive. A generally better-educated populace results in many positive social impacts that we all enjoy such as reduced crime and homelessness, increased tax revenue, and all types of advances to society that the educated among us achieve.

But negative externalities, like air pollution and the resultant impacts on climate change, represent an existential threat to humankind. Climate change is the physical science spinoff of externalities. Similarly, the degradation of water and land resources worldwide that escape the economic accounting system threaten to have almost as serious a detrimental impact on humanity as air pollution is now having. The quantity of potable water available for people in many countries around the world and within regions of the United States is becoming an acute problem. The degradation of arable land worldwide resulting in growing losses of topsoil stands to seriously impair the world's ability to grow sufficient food to meet the needs of growing populations (Ewaran, et al., 2001).

Externalities can be viewed as two different types. The first type might be appropriately called *accidental externalities.* These are externalities that spill over from an activity that might go unnoticed for a long time by everyone. The existence of these accidental externalities is a function of time and "the times." Air pollution associated with burning coal is an example. When the Industrial Revolution began in Britain in the late 1700s and early 1800s, manufacturing production began to increase rapidly. The bulk of that production was powered by more burning of coal as the revolution progressed. Water power used to mill grains and turn machinery in the factory could no longer supply enough power to keep the wheels of the Industrial Revolution turning, so coal was turned to for the production of steam power. The degradation of the air quality in London became so pronounced that Parliament began passing laws to deal with it by the mid-1800s (Ritchie, 2017). The negative impacts from these highly visible air pollutants were not only plain to see but began to have serious impacts on the breathability of air in the urban areas and the health of the people living in those areas. The detrimental impacts of these visible particulates, soot and smog, were inescapable. Steps began to be taken to mitigate these negative impacts. Laws were passed and regulations promulgated that began to address the more visible aspects of air pollution.

Similar to air pollution in nineteenth century in England,

water pollution became a serious problem in the twentieth century in the United States. The seemingly endless supply of clean water available in the US in the abundant lakes and rivers led to growing abuse of water resources. Rivers were often used, and in cases still are, as open sewers for factories and cities—pollutants piped directly into lakes by industrial plants. An awakening about the squandering of water resources finally took place in the 1960s. When the surface of the water in the Cuyahoga River in Ohio actually began to burn in 1969, it attracted national attention, becoming a cover story in *Time* magazine. The river had been ablaze a number of times prior to 1969, 1952 being the most damaging fire on the river, but the fire of 1969 captured national attention (at least the attention of someone who happened to be paying attention, which turned into national attention). In part because of that event, the Clean Water Act was passed in the United States and the Environmental Protection Agency was born.

Externalities exist in many areas of the economy, but the existence of externalities and their relation to various types of air, water, and land pollution are having some of the most significant impacts from an economic and social standpoint. As air pollution increases, health impacts mount, people suffer more breathing and heart problems, the incidence of asthma has been shown to increase, global temperatures rise and sea levels rise with them, plant and animal species become extinct, land mass disappears under the rising ocean levels, and catastrophic storms and droughts become more common. The costs associated with these consequences escape the micro-accounting systems of individual enterprises and also escape the macro-accounting at the state, national, and international levels. Many of these externalities might be viewed as accidental because for some period, long periods in some cases, the existence and impacts of these events go unnoticed, unrealized.

The other type of externality, somewhat different than accidental externalities, can be considered an *opportunistic externality*. The difference in these two types of externalities lie largely in time, timing, and technology. When coal was being burned in the early days of the Industrial Revolution, the knowledge and sophistication of the physical sciences was primitive. There was little understanding of the damage the soot and particulate matter from coal could have on the human lungs and heart—and even less knowledge about the long-term effects on the air quality of the earth's atmosphere on a global level.

Remember, it was only 200 years prior to this that Galileo convinced scientists that the earth revolved around the sun and not vice versa. Climatology was not close to being an advanced science. Hence, accidental externalities, the creation of by-product costs that are not actually seen or measurable with existing technology, can arise. The crudeness of technology in existence at points in history to find the spillovers, identify them, and then quantify them and their impacts, resulted in the creation of these accidental externalities.

Opportunistic externalities on the other hand are those known to exist and lend themselves to some level of measurement and economic quantification. Timing is everything. In England in the 1700s, the science of air pollution was restricted to what the naked eye could see or the nose could smell coming from the smokestacks of coal-fired industries. As these spillovers were recognized, laws were passed in an attempt to deal with the problem. Some of those laws merely required moving the sources of the coal-burning factories further from urban areas. At the time, no one knew anything about SO_2 or CO_2. Since the spillover was perceived as a problem restricted close to the source of the polluter, the answer was simple: move it downwind and further away. Science no longer allows such simple, inexpensive, and ineffective ways of dealing with most externalities.

When an externality is known to exist, but its existence is disingenuously disputed, when the costs are amenable to some level of quantification but assigning those costs is resisted, the externality becomes opportunistic. Advancements in science and technology will continue to limit the ability of true accidental externalities to arise. The existence of spillover effects in both production and consumption is becoming more susceptible to understanding and prediction and often to at least some rudimentary quantification.

The externalities associated with the production of, and hence the other side of the coin, consumption of, energy are some of the most insidious of externalities embedded in the US economic system, though they are by no means alone. The proliferation of electronic devices such as cellphones, computers, flat screen TVs, etc., are another slice of the economy where externalities are running wild. These devices require large amounts of heavy metals in their production. The mining and refining of these metals take place largely in Third World countries and China. Vast amounts of land must be dug up to produce exceedingly small amounts of these metals. The pure forms of these rare-earth metals are extracted from low-density ores by very environmentally degrading processes, in some cases leaching the metals from the ores with toxins, such as arsenic, that then find their way back into the groundwater and soil.

The degradation of the land, air, and water of the countries that serve as the supply shelf for these difficult-to-extract commodities is not figured into the price of the iPhone. If the cost of cleaner production of the heavy metals and remediation of natural resources after the mining was completed were figured into the cost of a new TV, the price would go up. Similarly, when old devices are retired, the costs associated with their recycling is not included in the cost of the device. When these electronic devices, which are being replaced at increasingly shorter intervals due both to technological innovation and marketing, are recycled, they are often loaded onto ships and end up in Third World countries where most of the content is just dumped into landfills (World Economic Forum, 2019). The cycle of pollution and resource degradation continues on in the graveyards of these devices.

Query: if the cost of a $900 iPhone was raised by say $200 to pay for remediation of the mining of the heavy-metal components

,and another $200 to actually recycle usable components and safely dispose of the remainder, resulting in a true cost of $1,300, would people buy as many iPhones or upgrade them as frequently? Likely not.

In economic terms, unless the price elasticity of demand for iPhones was zero, the number of iPhones demanded would drop, probably precipitously. Economics gets this part of the question right. The market understands the relationship between the price of a good and the number of units consumers will buy. The market does not deal very well with the externalities, and too often goes out of its way to ignore them . . . opportunistic externalities.

Returning to the energy industry as of 2019, 23 percent of power generated in the US came from coal while 38 percent was produced by burning natural gas (US EIA, 2020). Natural gas is replacing coal at a breakneck pace due to the falling cost of natural gas. Nevertheless, the acolytes of the coal industry have coined the phrase "clean coal," an oxymoronic chimera that does not exist (Winberg, 2020). Coal is the dirtiest fuel utilized for energy production. It produces more particulate matter, sulfur dioxide, and carbon dioxide than any other form of energy per BTU produced (Keating, 2001).

Coal is touted as the cheapest source of energy available to the US economy, but it is clear that all of the costs associated with the mining and burning of coal are not getting priced into the energy that comes from coal, particularly the price of air pollution. The East Coast and New England states have suffered for years from the accounting shortfalls of the coal industry and have attempted to make the industry "internalize" its externalities. In the 1960s the effects of acid rain, a result of the SO_2 produced by burning coal, began to show up in lakes in New England (Beasley, 2007). More and more lakes could no longer support fish life. Then in the 1990s, the problems with the particulate matter from coal plants in the Midwest and Ohio River Valley, which were carried east by the prevailing winds, began to impair eastern states' ability to meet air quality guidelines set out by the EPA. Eastern states banded together to sue utilities in the middle part of the country to force them to clean up their operations. This is the very definition of an externality: an Ohio utility sells it electricity to the residents of Ohio while sending its air pollutants off to New York and Vermont for those states to deal with. New York and Vermont were forced to impose restrictions on automobiles and industrial facilities in their states in order to accommodate the additional air pollution coming their way from utilities to their west.

The existence and perpetuation of externalities is anathema to the very core concept of the US notions of free-market capitalism. Why? The market is touted to be a mechanism that captures the costs of production, rolls them into the price of the good or service being provided, and offers the product to consumers who will then purchase the commodity in quantities reflective of the price of the commodity in relation to prices of similar competing products. If the price of one commodity is artificially held down because all of the costs of producing the commodity are not included in the price, the demand for that commodity will be artificially inflated . . . think flat-screen TVs and coal-generated electricity.

There are no doubt externalities yet to be uncovered in materials that will find their way into new products. In time we may discover that a chemical put into a product has significant spillover effects (costs) in production. Hopefully when those spillover costs are discovered, they will be built into the cost model. These true "accidental externalities" will continue to arise from time to time. Arguably with advancing technology, accidental externalities will be fewer and fewer as identification of externalities becomes easier and arise earlier in the product-development process. Externalities are not going to disappear anytime soon, but those that remain will increasingly become opportunistic externalities—nothing more than unfair attempts to increase profits and circumvent the market, ill-gotten gains. Nothing more, nothing less.

When externalities permeate the market, the market cannot

possibly perform the task it theoretically does. When prices do not reflect true costs, demand cannot reflect true consumer preferences. The whole system breaks down. The market becomes an arbitrary and capricious system in which those producers who are most adept at passing on their real costs to someone else win the game or have the highest profit margins.

Consider: If the cost of huge outputs of CO_2 into the environment were priced into coal, would it be as cheap or cheaper energy than wind or solar energy?

If the release of carbon into the atmosphere associated with massive strip-mining of tar sands in Alberta, Canada, were included in the cost of the oil by-product, would that oil be cheaper energy than wind, solar, or thermal? Or competitive with oil produced many other places?

If the costs to the health of native Ecuadorans, to their water and land, created by mining copper, zinc, and lead were fully imputed to the flat-screen TVs that require them, would as many Americans be able to afford 70-inch TVs to watch the Super Bowl?

If the costs associated with intense fertilization of Midwest farmland to produce abundant and cheap corn and soybeans, which results in a dead zone in the Gulf of Mexico the size of Rhode Island (NOAA, 2019), were included in the price of beef, poultry, and Cheerios, would consumers buy the same amount of these food products?

The answer to all these questions is of course, "No."

Scientists can identify most of these types of externalities. Economists need to price them. Greater efforts need to be spent by economists in developing pricing mechanisms that bring externalities of all types into the costs of production as easily as labor, cost of debt, and taxes. As long as massive spillovers escape the market's radar and go unpriced, the market is nothing more than a contrived charade greatly benefiting those who hide or transfer their true costs—and burdening those downstream who bear those costs.

CHAPTER 6

GDP

A Problem in the Metrics

I've discussed the US economic system and examined components of that system along with widely accepted notions of how the US economy functions, or how we think it functions. This next topic is not a component of the economy but rather the capstone of what the system does.

What do all of the myriad parts of the US economic system produce?

What comes out at the end of the process?

What does the capitalistic system of the United States produce?

What does the communist system of Russia produce?

How about China's government-directed system?

The outputs, the end product of all of these systems, are of course measured and compared. Gross Domestic Product (GDP) is the tool, the metric that has evolved to evaluate every economic system. So while GDP is not a piece of the economic machine, it is extremely important as the tool we use to monitor and evaluate all components of the system to track how they are working. In a

Rank	Country/Territory	GDP (US$million)
	World	**83,844,988**
1	United States	20,807,269
2	China	14,860,775
3	Japan	4,910,580
4	Germany	3,780,553
5	United Kingdom	2,638,296
6	India	2,592,583
7	France	2,551,451
8	Italy	1,848,222
9	Canada	1,600,264

(2020 estimates)

Figure 12. GDP by country 2019. *Source: International Monetary Fund*

sense, GDP has something to say about how the entire system is functioning and hence, by extension, how the various components add to the outcome.

GDP is the tool with which we measure our economy, and almost all nations use this same metric or a close variant. The ranking of the size of the world's economies are measured using GDP. Figure 12 shows the ranking of the world's largest economies as published by the International Monetary Fund (IMF, 2019).

The US economy is 50 percent larger than China's, four times larger than Japan's, and five times larger than Germany's. But what does that really tell us? The level of activity in the US economy is 1.5 times the level of economic activity in China. The US produces 50 percent more goods and services than China.

Is that a good thing? Somewhat.

Is that in important thing? Somewhat.

The answer is "somewhat" because GDP measures activity—not outcomes. A simple analogy might be to say that the US spends more time doing homework than anyone else in the class, but it does not say the US is the top student in the class. It says the US spends more money on healthcare than anyone else; it does not say Americans are the healthiest people on the planet (The World Bank, 2018). It tells us that the US spends more on highways and transit systems than anyone else in the world except China (OECD, 2020), but it does not tell us the US transportation system is better than everyone's but China. It tells us the US spends more money on public safety, court systems, and prisons than any other country, but does not tell us that US streets and neighborhoods are the safest in the world. The US GDP tells us the US spends more on and produces more recreation (boats, ATVs, movies, computer games, theme parks) than any other country; but it gives no indication that Americans are happier than anyone else in the world. The US expenditures on food per capita are among the highest in the world (USDA, 2017), but it does not tell us if the food Americans eat is better or Americans are healthier than anyone else on earth. GDP tells us how fast the treadmill is going; but it fails to tell if we are actually getting anywhere.

There are two widely used ways to define the US GDP, one based on consumption and the other on production. The most widely used formula is in terms of consumption: GDP= C + I + G + E. This formulation tells us who buys the goods and services the US economic engine produces, everything produced by the economy is either *consumed* by individuals (C), it is *invested* in business enterprises such as machinery and buildings (I), it is purchased by federal, state, and local *government* (G), or it is purchased by parties outside the borders of the US (net *exports*; exports minus imports, E).

GDP is the metric used to measure the world economies. Much has been written about shortcomings of that measurement tool. I do not dwell on that extensively here, but it is a major problem plaguing the US market system, so it merits some discussion. For a more-detailed discussion of issues associated with GDP globally, I suggest an excellent book by Amartya Sen, Jean Paul Fitoussi, and Joseph Stiglitz, *Mismeasuring our Lives: Why GDP Doesn't Add Up* (The New York Press, 2010).

Measurement schemes are important in everything we do. We strive to improve the numbers in whatever we are measuring; greater earnings per share, greater output per hour of input, increasing individual net worth, lower body mass index, more miles of roads paved per dollars spent, and more ton-miles of rail freight hauled per gallon of fuel expended. Whatever we measure (and we measure everything), we work to "improve the numbers." So too with GDP; we strive to grow the GDP. One of the most highly watched and highly regarded measures of a country's well-being is its GDP per capita.

It is ironic that as time goes on and we think of the US economy and markets gaining sophistication, the US financial markets are becoming more quantitative and complex; US corporate accounting systems are more fine-tuned, accurate, and descriptive; and the level of sophistication with which we measure the US national economy remains crude to say the least. GDP measures what is produced (goods and services). It does not come close to capturing the costs associated with that output. If a corporate CFO went to a financial institution to seek funding armed with half an income statement and no balance sheet, they would immediately be shown the door. Yet at a national level that is the equivalent of the degree of precision and sophistication we often apply to the US economy. Since GDP is the measuring tool, that is what every country strives to increase: the raw number. When US GDP shrinks, or grows at a lower than expected rate, financial markets drop. When China's GDP grew at a rate of 9 percent or greater, markets all over the world were lifted in response to China's growth rate.

What GDP is comprised of is not focused on in detail by most people. There is some interest in how much of the total GDP is created by export activity (E) and how much is composed of domestic consumption (C), in part to analyze the sustainability of the growth rate, but little attention is paid to how that incremental increase in economic output has actually gone to improve the lot of anyone in the country. With over $100 billion added to the US GDP in 2016 by the tobacco industry, is the US better off as a country?[7] If that number could be doubled to $200 billion would that be desirable? GDP would be larger. The financial industry's share of corporate profits has risen steadily for decades; peaking at 40 percent of total profits in 2004 just before the financial collapse that lead to the Great Recession (Weissmann, 2014). That did not seem to work out too well for the US economy. A few more detailed examples will sharpen the focus on the problem:

After a large catastrophic event like hurricane Katrina, a tremendous amount of money is spent rebuilding the wreckage. Armies of carpenters, electricians, excavators, bricklayers, insurance adjusters, engineers, etc., are employed in the reconstruction process. In addition, a huge amount of raw material goes into the process: lumber, cement, wiring, window glass, asphalt, landscaping material, and on and on. The value of all of this adds to GDP. An event like this could easily add several billion dollars to the US economic output. Granted there will also be some lost output of businesses impacted by the hurricane. Businesses will be shut down and suffer lost production during the rebuilding effort. But that aside, what was the effect of the hurricane? It provided a temporary jolt to GDP as a massive reconstruction effort was undertaken. New Orleans existed before Katrina; New Orleans existed after Katrina. The US did not gain a new city. The US balance sheet did not grow (Sweet, 2017). We had a Gulf port city before and after the storm. Essentially the national balance sheet did not change. The economy theoretically grew but the asset base, upgrades, and enhancements aside, remained the same. The national income accounts did not count the human suffering, the lost educational time for the children in the city, the reduction in natural resources

7. Grandview Research. Competitive Landscape And Segment Forecasts, 2018–2025.

that went into the reconstruction (Flowers, 2018). The rebuilding activity following Katrina, or any natural disaster, is reflected in GDP much like economic activity is reported on an income statement; there is no balance sheet counterpart in GDP calculations. Nonetheless, the economy grew—or did it?

Another set of data further illustrates the point about what GDP does and does not tell us. Figure 13 shows the level of GDP just preceding and through the war years of World War II (1939–1945) and the Korean War (1949–1953). In 1939 the US was still coming out of the Depression, but war had broken out in Europe. Economic activity in the US grew dramatically as the production of ships, airplanes, munitions, and support materials of many types were ramped up. The US economy grew at 18–19 percent rates for several years during World War II, rates unheard of over the previous sixty years. Similarly, when the Korean War broke out, it pulled the US economy out of recession in 1949 and jumped-started the economy for the next two years. Again production of war material increased dramatically, and any slack in the labor markets was rapidly absorbed by the war effort. What happened to the output of the revved-up economic engine during those years? Much of what was built—ships, tanks, aircraft—was quickly destroyed in combat. Much of what was not destroyed in combat was eventually brought back to the US and mothballed or scrapped or decommissioned in one manner or another. Much of the asset base created during these years was used to destroy assets in other parts of the world, namely Europe and Asia. Housing, commercial buildings, rail lines, utilities, schools, hospitals were destroyed on massive scales. The level of asset destruction in Europe brought about changes to their economies that are still being dealt with.

So what do the high economic growth rates during World War II and the Korean War tell us about GDP? Were people in the US better off? Rationing of basic commodities was taking place. Young people were not attending college. Auto companies were

Year	Real GDP	Growth
1939	$1.164	8.0%
1940	$1.266	8.8%
1941	$1.490	17.7%
1942	$1.772	18.9%
1943	$2.074	17.0%
1944	$2.239	8.0%
1945	$2.218	-1.0%
1949	$2.009	-0.5%
1950	$2.184	8.7%
1951	$2.360	8.1%
1952	$2.456	4.1%
1953	$2.571	4.7%

Source: Federal Reserve Bank of St. Louis

Figure 13. US GDP growth during WWII and the Korean War

building tanks rather than cars. The loss of life was enormous. Those were some of the impacts on the US. In Europe and Asia, the US economic activity was helping to destroy entire cities with the associated human suffering on a leviathan scale.

A final perspective on looking at US economic activity through the lens of GDP: the United States incarcerates more people than any other country on earth. The US incarceration rate is 737 per 100,000 people. Russia's is 615 per 100,000. China's rate is only 118 per 100,000. The total US prison population is slightly over 2,000,000 while China's prison population is only 1.7 million, even though China has a population three times that of the US (World Population Review, 2020).

Much of the prison system in the US is publicly operated, but a growing part of it is built and operated by private companies.

Several large corporate prison operations make up the bulk of the for-profit prison industry including companies like Core Civic, formerly Corrections Corporation of America. In 2019 this for-profit prison company had almost $2 billion in revenue.[8] So how does the penal system affect the US GDP? When the prisons are built the construction adds to the GDP: materials, manufactured products, construction workers' salaries. Once the prison is built, the salaries of the law enforcement agencies, court systems, and huge staffs to operate the facilities all add to GDP. One could be somewhat cynical and say that this is a niche market which allows the US to grow GDP. A slight adjustment in various areas of the criminal code, moving some gross misdemeanors into the felony category, could help grow the GDP. But while many elements of the US criminal justice system "add" to the economy, what are we missing with this kind of crude calculation?

First of all, the economy overall loses due to a lack of earning power of the prison population. Lost productivity of people taken out of the economy (having two million people locked up) and the foregone tax revenue are all missed in the calculations. The costs associated with trying to get these people back into the mainstream of society as they leave prison are measured. The salaries of social workers and other rehabilitative staff are tallied, but the US does not tally the losses to individuals and their lives of having these people in prison, nor is there a calculation of the opportunity cost of having people taken out of society for years: loss of job skills, loss of demand to the total economy, kids who will suffer a great deal over the course of their lives because they had a parent behind bars instead of attending school conferences and helping them with homework each night. If those two million people were each earning $25,000 per year, the economy would have an annual boost of $50 billion in income and, commensurately, demand. Crude calculations pick up what the penal system adds to the economy, but

8. Market Watch. Annual Financials for CoreCivic Inc.

it does not even attempt to capture the losses due to having two million people behind bars.

More attention has focused on measuring economies over the past few years, but much more work remains to be done. The tiny country of Bhutan began years ago measuring its economy by a measure called the GNHI, Gross National Happiness Index, rather than the standard GDP. Bhutan, a small Asian country of less than two million people and a GDP of $9 billion, compared to the $19 trillion of US GDP, promulgated their Gross National Happiness Index in 2008. While far from a panacea of how to measure a country's progress, well-being, or state of sustainability, the Index represented a step in a far different direction than GDP moves.

The GNHI is built upon "four pillars": 1) sustainable and equitable socioeconomic development, 2) environmental conservation, 3) preservation and promotion of culture, and 4) good governance. Under these four pillars are nine domains of psychological well-being: health, time use, education, cultural diversity and resilience, good governance, community vitality, ecological diversity and resilience, and living standards (GNH Centre Bhuton). Efforts in Bhutan to take stock of their economy in a different way than Western economies may have a quasi-spiritual, kumbaya feel to some. The efforts by this tiny country have been studied and in some respects replicated elsewhere. The European Union developed the European Statistical System, an effort to measure quality of life in EU countries and well-being of their citizens (Eurostat, 2019). The World Bank has developed the Human Development Index (HDI) to measure quality of life indices in countries, by which index the US ranks fifteenth in the world (UNDP, 2019). In 2019 New Zealand unveiled a new national budgeting process that requires every national department to focus on measures of well-being for the country as they each develop their budgets (Samuel, 2019).

The common thread in these nascent efforts is an attempt to get a more meaningful measure of the pulse, the blood pressure, the cholesterol level, if you will, of a country's economy. GDP tells us just one thing, how much activity is going on in the economy. It fails to tell us where that activity is taking us or what impact all of that activity is having on everything around us; the well-being of people, the state of natural resources, the declining biodiversity of the environment, the sustainability of economic activity. Measuring something as complex and composed of the many moving parts as a national economy poses huge challenges. A reading of the book by Sen, Fitoussi, and Stiglitz gives one a grasp of the complexity of the issues that must be dealt with in measuring an economy and some of the differing conceptual approaches that can be used. For example, just applying basic accounting notions to the economy, much like we do to individual businesses, raises challenging questions. How do we begin to measure all those things that belong on a national balance sheet? The quantity and quality of labor stock? The stocks of natural resources, water, timber, untapped metals, clean air, tillable soil, diversity in the ecosystem? Yet these are exactly the types of calculations that must be made to measure in a very rudimentary way whether we are adding to a national balance sheet or depleting the ability to sustain a level of economic activity very far into the future. If US water resources are consumed too fast and not allowed to replenish, the US loses the ability to support the population with water to drink, bathe, and recreate; if the US labor force is not adequately added to by sufficient investment in education, the US loses the ability to innovate, make medical breakthroughs, create quality of life improving devices, add to musical, literary, and artistic treasures; if US soil is so degraded by loss of topsoil or excessive application of chemicals, the country loses the ability to sustain the food supply; if US air is continually polluted, the country may even lose the ability to inhabit the planet in any way that Americans have become accustomed to.

It bears repeating, we focus on improving that which we measure; hence the importance of getting it right when we develop the metrics. If we get it wrong, we might find ourselves in another 100 years with a GDP that has grown tenfold but, with land so degraded that famine is widespread, clean water so scarce that it has become the resource countries go to war over, air so polluted that everyone wears face makes when outside and temperatures have warmed to catastrophic levels, and the lack of investment in human stock has been so low that the level of technological innovation has ground to a halt. While none of this needs to happen, far greater attention must be paid to measuring all facets of the US ecosystem to avoid it. The economics departments of universities in the US, and around the world, need to be unleashed on improving the metrics. A reemphasis on studying and thinking about the fundamentals of the US system is needed. To a degree, the more analytical work in such areas as finance, behavioral economics, econometrics, etc., implicitly assumes that the core of the US economic model is satisfactory. The core needs to be rethought and one of the most fundamental places to start is in the way to measure the complex interrelated processes taking place in the US economic system.

CHAPTER 7

INCOME AND WEALTH DISPARITY

An Existential Threat to Society

There is no dispute that the distribution of income and wealth in the United States and many other developed countries is becoming more and more skewed. Much has been written about this topic in recent years. The numbers depicting wide and growing dipartites in income and wealth between segments of the population are at our fingertips. The question germane to this discussion is: What does wealth disparity have to do with a critique of the US "free market" system?

Economic inequality is not a component of the US system. It is not a component of the "market" as are information or demand. Economic inequality does not describe how parts of the system relate to one another as externalities do. It is not a metric held out to quantify the system, as is GDP. Wealth disparity is nothing more than one by-product of the US economic system: the market. In addition to goods and services and everything else the US economy produces, it generates income and wealth distribution. Income and wealth distribution do not happen in a vacuum. No predetermined wealth distribution is automatically generated regardless of changes we make to the system. Economic inequality comes about as result of tax policy, access to quality education, access to affordable healthcare, legal constructs, governmental regulatory schemes, political philosophies, and a myriad of other factors. In a sense, economic equality, or lack thereof, might be viewed as the "canary in the coal mine" for any economic system—certainly if one views the level of equality or inequality as an indicator of the overall health of the system that generates the outcome.

Some might say it really does not matter how wealth is distributed among a population; it is what it is. They might argue that the market is producing whatever outcome it is destined to create. Not so. Wealth distribution does matter; it matters a great deal. There are serious implications for society as a result of income disparities that can be viewed through at least three lenses: economic, social, and moral. All three perspectives highlight various ramifications for society. Income disparity and wealth disparity are two different things which we will discuss in more detail, and yet, in a sense, they are two different ways of looking at and measuring the same thing: well-being disparity.

A discussion of the skewed distribution of income and wealth in the US starts with a clear and simple recitation of the reality of the issue. Dealing first with income distribution, we look at the extent of the maldistribution, the direction it is headed, and the speed with which it is changing. By 2016 approximately 50 percent of the income earned in the country went to the top 10 percent of income earners. The top 1 percent of income earners took home about 25 percent of the national income (Stone, et al., 2020).

In contrast to recent years, the share of income earned by those at the top was relatively stable and much lower from the end of World War II until about 1982. That number began to steadily in-

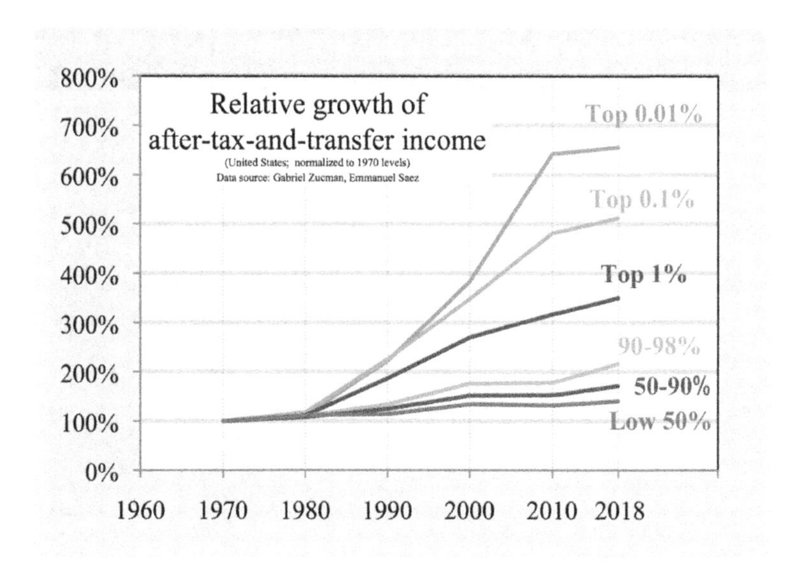

Figure 14. 2018 Household income percentiles

crease from 1982 and in 2020 stood at about 50 percent of total income. The data can be parsed and described in many different ways, but the bottom line is that more and more income is going to a smaller and smaller percentage of the total population. Hence inequality is increasing dramatically. Over the last forty years, the real income of the middle 60 percent of US wage earners has remained constant at around $50,000 per person. Over the same period the top 1 percent of income earners saw their income rise in real terms from about $300,000 per year to over $1,250,000 per year—an increase of over 300 percent, again in real terms. What might be considered the middle class has seen no increase in their income in inflation adjusted terms.

Figure 14 clearly depicts the extremely skewed distribution of income in the US. Income growth is fairly constant across the lower 70 to 80 percent of incomes. Once you move above the 80 percentile, incomes start to rise quickly and at an increasing rate, shown by the huge spike in income at the 99th percentile to almost

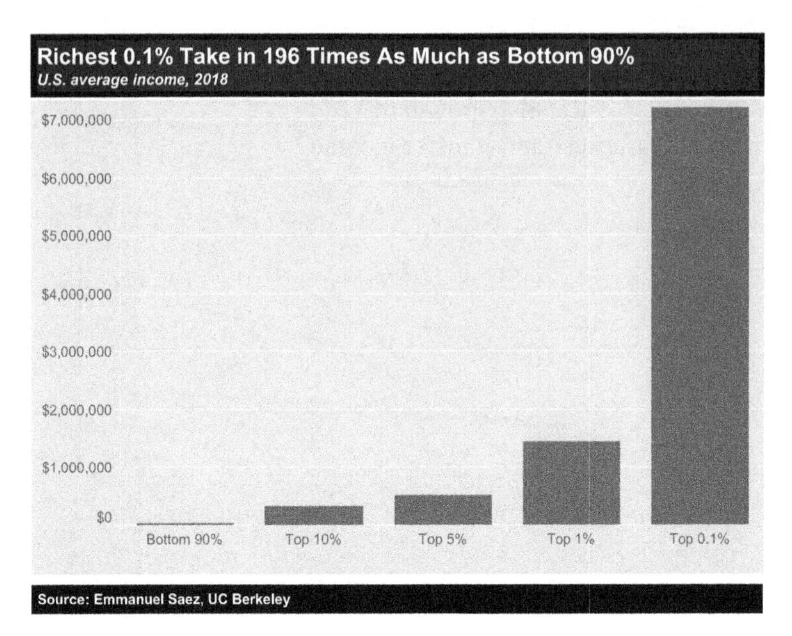

Figure 15. Income by income percentiles

$500,000 per year. This provides a snapshot of where income distribution is in the US.

An even more disturbing picture of the income distribution issue starts to take shape when you look at the stratification taking place at the very top of the income pyramid. Figure 15, prepared by Emmanuel Saez, looks at income in the top 10 percent, 5 percent, 1 percent, and .1 percent. While the top 10 percent of earners are making around $200,000 per year, the top 0.1 percent are earning over $7,000,000 per year. Disparity takes on a whole new meaning when we begin slicing the pie into smaller and smaller groups at the top. These figures show that 167,000 household earned 196 times as much as 150,000,000 households combined.

A look back at Figure 14 gives some clues as to how and when this income disparity became so pronounced. As Figure 14 depicts, in the early 1980's the growth in incomes of those in the top 1%

of earners began to rise dramatically along with more subdued income growth in the top half of the population. This coincides with the beginning of a long period of income tax reductions that have continued up until as recently as 2017.

The top income levels began to increase significantly around 1980. What factors caused these income differences to widen so significantly? This has been attributed to a confluence of events including a decline in union membership (i.e. lower wage growth for lower and middle-income earners) and the start of the steady decline in income tax rates.

The statistics clearly reveal huge and widening disparities in wealth distribution. Another important and widely used indicator of income inequality is the Gini coefficient. The Gini coefficient is a mathematical construct that measures the degree of variance between perfect equality of distribution among any population characteristic (in this case income) and the observed distribution. A Gini coefficient equal to 0 would indicate perfectly equal distribution of the characteristic being examined. A Gini coefficient of 1 indicates a totally unequal distribution of income. For example, if the lowest 20 percent of the population owns 20 percent of the wealth, and the lowest 60 percent of the population holds 60 percent of the wealth, then there is no inequality. Wealth is distributed evenly. The Gini coefficient is 0.

On the other hand, if there is a population of 100 people, and 1 person holds all of the wealth, there is total inequality of distribution; the Gini coefficient for this distribution is 1 (OECD, 2006). Thus the higher the Gini coefficient is for a population, the greater the inequality of the distribution. One of the strong points of the Gini coefficient is that it allows for inter-country comparisons of the distribution of wealth at any point in time. It also allows the measurement over time within a country of wealth distribution. There are of course some issues with the data that go into the calculation. Data differ somewhat between countries, and methods

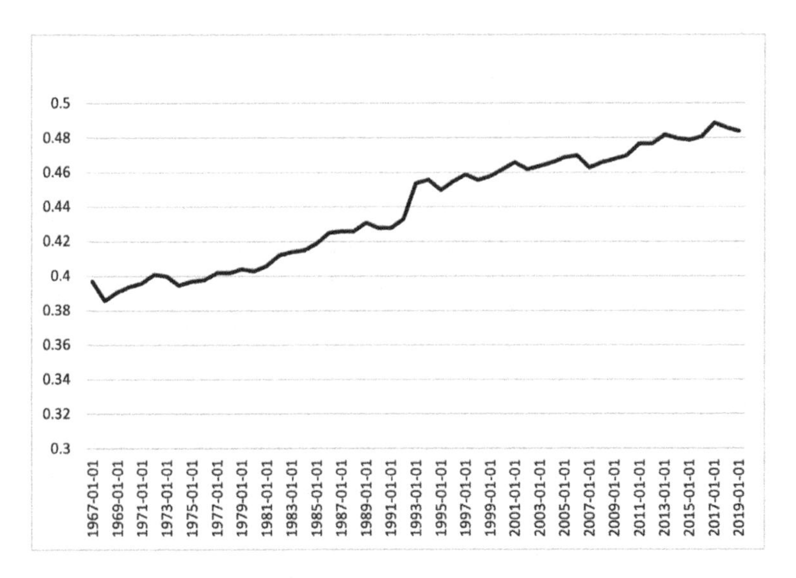

Figure 16. Gini Coefficient of Income in the US

---

of calculation can differ over time within a country. Nevertheless it offers a good and relatively equal comparison of data over time and between countries.

So what does the Gini coefficient say about income distribution in the United States? Figure 16 depicts the Gini coefficient of income distribution in the US from 1967 up to 2019, as compiled by the Federal Reserve Bank of St. Louis.

The graph shows that the Gini coefficient for income has grown from .37 in 1968 to .48 where it currently lies (the higher the number, the more unequal the distribution of the characteristic being measured). The upward trend of the line is obvious, indicating the steadily increasing inequality of how income is distributed across the population. Note that the upward slope of the line has increased since the early 1980s. Remember that in 1982, the highest marginal tax rate was cut from 70 to 50 percent under President Reagan, and thus began the long thirty-year descent of the highest marginal tax rate to the 37 percent in effect in 2020.

As we saw earlier from Figure 14, income began to be much more unevenly distributed in the early 1980s with that trend continuing to the present time. How do these Gini coefficient numbers compare with other parts of the world? The Scandinavian countries and much of Western Europe, including Germany, have Gini coefficients in the range of .25-.29. Canada, India, and the remainder of Western Europe have income distributions between .30-.34. Countries with income distributions even more skewed than the US (Gini coefficients .5 and >) include much of Latin America, Russia, sub-Saharan Africa, and South Africa (Ventura, 2018).

Volumes of data are compiled by legions of federal agencies, think tanks, and economists, which have been presented in dozens of formats. The data all says the same thing. It is irrefutable. Income distribution in the US has become absurdly unequal over the past forty years. This did not happen by chance; it has happened by design.

A look at wealth disparity reveals an even more skewed picture. Thirty years ago, the highest 1 percent of wealth holders in the US held 25 percent of the wealth; by 2019 they owned 40 percent of the country's wealth (Clemens, 2019). Wealth has been transferred significantly and quickly into fewer and fewer hands. The income and wealth distributions in the United States became far more equitable after the early part of the twentieth century, the famed gilded age, and leveled off at those levels for the next forty years following the end of World War II.

We are again approaching the uneven wealth distributions not seen in the US in almost 100 years. Over the past fifty years, the share of wealth held by the highest net worth people in the country (top 1 percent) has not changed dramatically. By far the largest increase in wealth has taken place in the top .01 percent of the population. Their wealth has grown from about 3 percent of the entire wealth in the US to around 12 percent. Bear in mind, this .01 percent is made up of about 30,000 people out of 330,000,000.

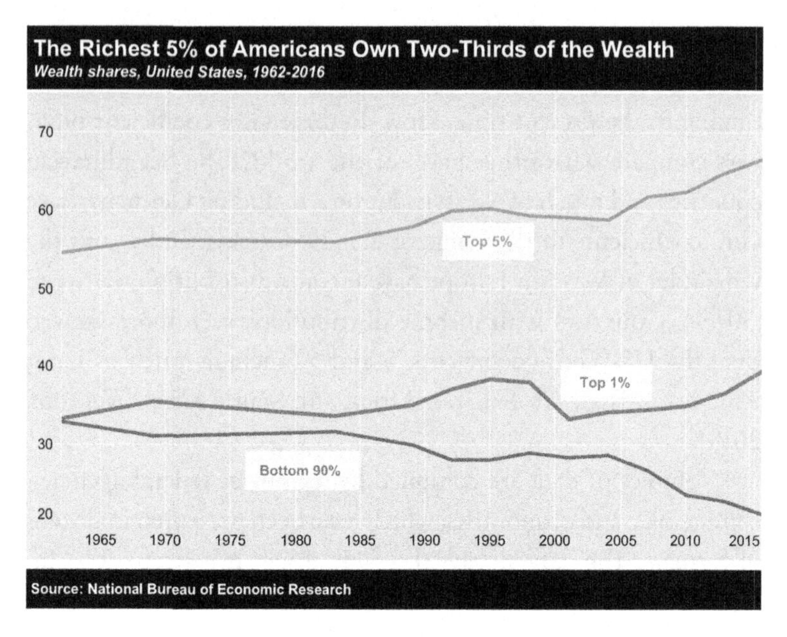

Figure 17. Wealth ownership in the US 1962-2016

If broken down to households, we are talking about less than half that number: fewer than 15,000 households nationwide. Meanwhile, the wealth owned by the bottom 90 percent of the US population has declined from just over 30 percent to less than 20 percent. Clearly the gains of those at the top have come at the expense of those at the bottom and those in the middle. Any way you look at it, a relatively tiny number of people in the US garner larger and larger shares of the economic pie.

The dramatic change in wealth distribution over the past half-century is evident in Figure 17. The general shape of wealth distribution did not change much from 1963 to 1983 . Then in the mid-1980s, ownership of wealth began to change dramatically. And the tail of the wealth curve at the 99th percentile of the population has stretched out significantly. Average family wealth in the 99th percentile tripled from 1983 to 2016; wealth for those in the bottom half of the population and below increased less than 20 percent. All of this serves as a starting point for further discussion.

As noted earlier, the inequitable distribution of wealth in the US is even greater than the inequity in income distribution, much greater. The top 1 percent of earners take home about 20 percent of national income. The top 1 percent of wealth holders in the US own about 40 percent of the wealth. Why does this uneven distribution of income and wealth matter? Or does it matter?

Economic inequality does matter! And it matters greatly for several reasons. There are three perspectives from which this massive maldistribution in income and wealth need to be examined: economic, social, and moral.

Economic Aspects of Inequality

When the lowest 20 percent of earners are making about $13,000 per year, and the next higher 20 percent of earners are making less than $40,000 per year, you have 40 percent of the population not earning enough money to get by, even at a marginal level. At those income levels, people spend most of their money on housing, food, and transportation. There is little left over for investments in themselves or their children (education), little left for entertainment and recreation, and nothing left for savings. At the lower-income levels most people rent their housing rather than own it. This results in lower-income people missing out on building equity in what is the largest single asset of most people in the US, their home.

Without the ability to buy a house, most people are unable to build any kind of positive net worth. For this cohort of the population, savings is not only impossible but going deeper and deeper into is debt is a way of life.

Figure 18 created by theFederal Reserve Bank of San Francisco, depicts the percentage of income spent on various expenditures by the lowest 20% of income earners. The lower-income groups

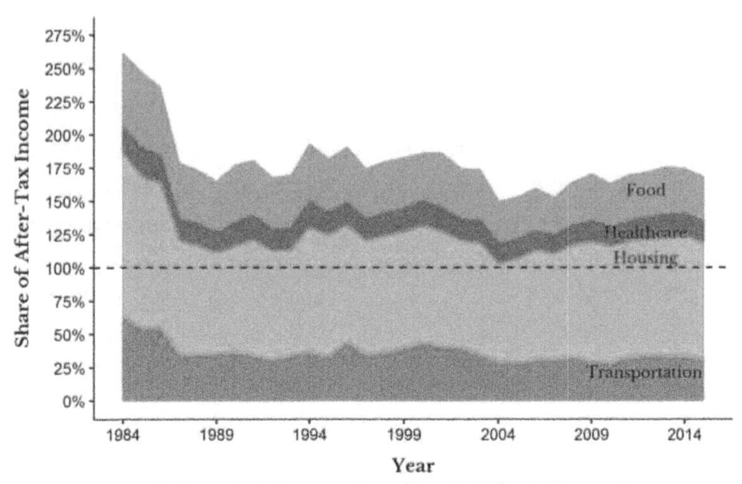

Figure 18. Consumption expenditures as percent of disposable income

spend more than they earn just on essentials: food, housing, utilities, transportation. These lower-income people either borrow or find other sources of income to supplement life's needs.

Seventy percent of the US economy is made up of consumer spending—spending on all items from durables (those items lasting more than three years) to services. What happened during the Great Recession that began in 2006 was a collapse in spending for several well-discussed reasons. As people lost jobs by the millions, and assets deflated in value at an extremely high rate of speed, consumers had less and less to spend on everything. To the extent that there was any concern about the pace of economic growth since the recession (but pre-COVID pandemic), it was not due to a lack of productive capacity or a lack of capital. The lessons being learned from the COVID-19-induced recession are similar.

While these two economic catastrophes are different in character and causes, the results are the same. Productive capacity was still standing, but as incomes collapsed there was drastically reduced ability to purchase what could be produced, either goods or services. The amount of cash and short-term deposits in banks that could conceivably be directed into investment opportunities, should they arise, is around $5 trillion (BOGMBASE, 2020). Capacity utilization rates in the US have been below 80 percent since the Great Recession and with the COVID pandemic have fallen below 70 percent (FRED, 2020). The problem is on the other side of the equation. There is insufficient demand for all types of goods and services to bring all that idle capital and capacity into the economy and be productively put to work.

Another fact of economic life is that people with different income levels have differing propensities to consume, i.e., the tendency to spend each incremental dollar of income that one has goes down the more income you have. Studies have estimated the marginal propensity to consume out of each incremental dollar at: from 0.6 for low-income people to 0.2 for high-income individuals. Studies look at that relationship in different ways, but generally low-income earners spend two to three times more additional income than high-income earners (Fisher, et al., 2019). Those in the bottom 50 percent of earners will spend everything they make on housing, food, transportation, education, and medical expenses. Those in the top 10 percent of earners will likely save 25–30 percent of every additional dollar they take in.

The top 1 percent is earning 25 percent of the national income (about $20 trillion/year) or approximately $5 trillion/year. If even 20 percent of that income was shifted to the lowest half of the income earners in the population, the entire $1 trillion might be spent, whereas with that income accruing to the top 1 percent, only about half is turning into effective demand for goods and services in the economy. An additional $500+ billion of spending would provide a significant boost for the economy (Fisher, et al, 2018). Putting $500 billion of additional spending on top of $14 trillion of current spending would have a noticeable impact. Again, what has held the economy back is lack of demand, not lack of supply.

Conversely, as the economy grows, and more incremental income is pushed into the hands of the highest income earners, aggregate demand does not get the boost it needs to sustain growth, as long as the US economy is fueled 70 percent by consumption spending. With an economy so heavily dependent on consumer spending, it behooves everyone to be sure consumers have enough money to spend to keep the engine running.

If income is shifted down the distribution curve from the top 1 percent, or top .1 percent to the bottom 50 percent, another change takes place. The character of demand changes. Consider a component of final demand like housing. If lower-income people have more money to spend on housing, builders will take notice. Affordable housing is in short supply in the US, in part because people needing affordable housing do not have enough money to buy inexpensive homes or rent modest, well-maintained housing. There is no shortage of very high-end housing in the US. The market fills that need quite nicely because plenty of people want that type of housing and have the money to pay for it. Similarly, for transportation spending, the lower third of income earners spend about 25 percent of their income on transportation of one form or another, primarily on cars. That is a higher percentage of income than generally thought to be reasonable to spend on transportation. Demand in the US economy is registered by having money in your pocket to spend on things. Without money, an individual becomes invisible to the market.

Shifting more of the national income from the very high income earners to those further down the income curve will result in the production of a different basket of goods and services geared to meet the demands of a different slice of the population. Look again at Figure 11. One way to think about it is this: as you move across the income spectrum, you define a unique basket of goods and services that are desired by that increment of people. As incomes go up, the composition of market demand for goods and services changes along with it. People earning $50,000 will desire and have a chance at affording houses costing $100,000–$200,000, and cars priced below $20,000. Individuals earning $1,000,000 will seek out houses costing several million dollars, and cars costing $50,000 to $100,000 or more.

From the supply side of the consumer market, it is easy to see where the first dollars will get invested. Whether analyzing housing, cars, clothing, food, or any consumer item, the profit margins are always higher the farther up the cost ladder one goes. The profit margin on a multimillion-dollar home is far higher than on a $200,000 newly constructed house. That is a large part of the reason builders have no problem putting a two-million-dollar home on an acre lot rather than subdividing it into four lots and building four much smaller homes on each lot.

The same economics apply to automobiles. Large SUVs are far more profitable for the automakers than small and medium-sized sedans. Reportedly Ford could earn $18,000 on one of its Ford Excursion SUVs but struggle to break even on the small Ford Focus (Hirsch 2020). The profit earned on a $15 T-shirt pales in comparison to that on a $300 dress shirt.

Profit margins on luxury goods are extremely large compared to the margins for all lower-end products. Capital will flow first to production of higher margin goods, i.e., capital will seek the highest return possible. By moving more income down the curve to lower-income people, the aggregate demand for less-expensive products will shift, and production will move to satisfy it.

Social Aspects of Inequality

For society, a massive and growing disparity in income and wealth is not healthy. Much has been written about the unrest and divisions it fosters among groups of people. A sense of the common good disappears as different groups feel their station in life is so far removed from others that common ground and common purpose are lost. As has happened in the US over the past thirty years, people are becoming more isolated from one another, divided largely along economic lines. People in different economic groups have less interaction with those in other economic strata. US schools are becoming divided into schools for the haves and the have-nots. Private schools continue to siphon off the more well-to-do students whose parents can afford private school tuition. While some disparity in income levels is certainly needed in the US market based economy to provide the incentives that many people need to work hard, innovate, create, move ahead and up the income ladder, there are limits to what is necessary to provide the psychological incentive to motivate people. There are points at which the disparities become highly destructive to a well-functioning society. Arguably the US is presently entering those ranges.

History tells us very graphically what happens when income and wealth are squirreled away at the top of the ladder, and the vast majority of people share in a very tiny percentage of the wealth of a country. At extreme levels of inequality, unrest results that ends in revolutions, often violent. The revolution in the US in the 1700s resulted from, among other factors, the economic oppression of the American colonists by the government of England. The revolution in France in the late 1700s, the Mexican Revolution in the early 1900s, the Russian Revolution in the early twentieth century, the revolutions in many Latin American countries in the 1950s (Cuba) through the 1980s (Nicaragua) have all been products of unrest caused by too few having too much, and too many having too little. The Cuban Revolution 90 miles from US shores in 1959 would not have happened had not a tiny percentage of the population controlled almost all the wealth in that country.

In 1905, a few years prior to the Russian Revolution, the top 1 percent of income earners took home about 13 percent of the total income of Russia (Nafziger & Lindert, 2012). In 2011, the year of the Arab Spring, the top 1 percent in Egypt took home 16 percent of the national income. In the US today, the top 1 percent take home 25 percent of the national income. In Cuba in 1953 the Gini coefficient for income was .57. In the years leading up the Arab Spring (2004) the Gini coefficient in Syria was .35; and in Egypt it was .32 (Index Mundi, 2019). The Gini coefficient for income in the US today is .48. The fact of the matter is that massive inequity is usually the igniting factor to revolution.

The World Factbook developed by the Central Intelligence Agency and referenced in the end notes shows a listing of Gini coefficients for income for most countries in the world. It should be noted that areas of the globe that are hotbeds of unrest tend to lie above the US in terms of income inequality (Gini coefficients higher than the US). These are countries in Africa and Latin America (Chetty, et al., 2014). Other factors can lead to societal unrest resulting in revolution, but certainly income inequity is an indicator of potential trouble for the tranquil functioning of a society. It is a "canary in the coal mine" for any society. By any measure, the economic inequality developing in the US is in ranges where discontent and unrest throughout history have reached the level that leads to cataclysmic shifts in societies. All countries, including the US, ignore this at their peril.

Moral Aspects of Inequality

The wealth of the US in aggregate terms is vast by any historical standard. The number of billionaires in the US continues to grow. According to *Forbes*, there were 607 billionaires in the US in 2018. Yet almost one-fourth of the children in the country live below the poverty line. Life expectancy is much shorter for those living at or below the poverty line than for those higher up on the income scale. The quality of life as measured by any factor—nutritional quality, access to quality education, access to medical care—is different for low-income people than those with greater incomes.

View this against the fact that income mobility in the United States is not terribly great. If you are born in the lower fifth of the income strata, your chances of moving several strata higher are not

Relative mobility is almost twice as high in Canada

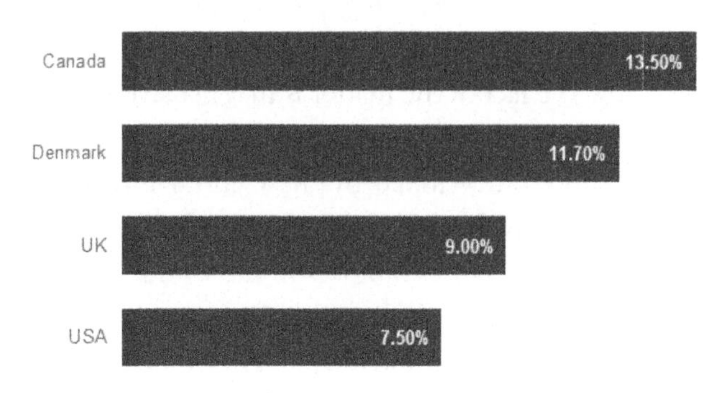

■ Probability that a child born to parents in the bottom fifth of the income distribution reaches the top fifth

Sources: Chetty et al., "Where is the land of opportunity? The geography of intergenerational mobility in the United States" (USA); Blanden and Machin, "Up and down the generational income ladder in Britain: Past changes and future prospects," (UK); Boserup, Kopczuk, and Kreiner, "Intergenerational Wealth Mobility: Evidence from Danish Wealth Records of Three Generations." (Denmark); Corak and Heisz, "The intergenerational earnings and income mobility of Canadian men: Evidence from longitudinal tax data" (Canada)

BROOKINGS

Figure 19. Mobility between income groups in US and peer countries

---

as great as one might like to think, nor is the chance that you will remain in the higher-income level even if you achieve it for a short while. Americans like to think that the US is a country where anyone can succeed, where everyone who wants to work hard can pull themselves up by their bootstraps. The facts say otherwise. While many people do move out of the lower-income strata and into higher levels, statistics tell us the majority do not. The fact is—you will very likely stay in about the same economic level into which you are born. And while income mobility may not be decreasing, it is certainly not increasing in the current environment. Where you are born in life will significantly dictate where you end up later in life. Quality of life and success in most respects is an accident of birth.

Harvard economist Raj Chetty has studied economic mobility extensively. Two graphic representations of his findings depict the friction that exists in moving between income strata in the US. Figure 19 shows the likelihood of being born in the bottom 20 percent of income earners and making it into the top 20 percent. The

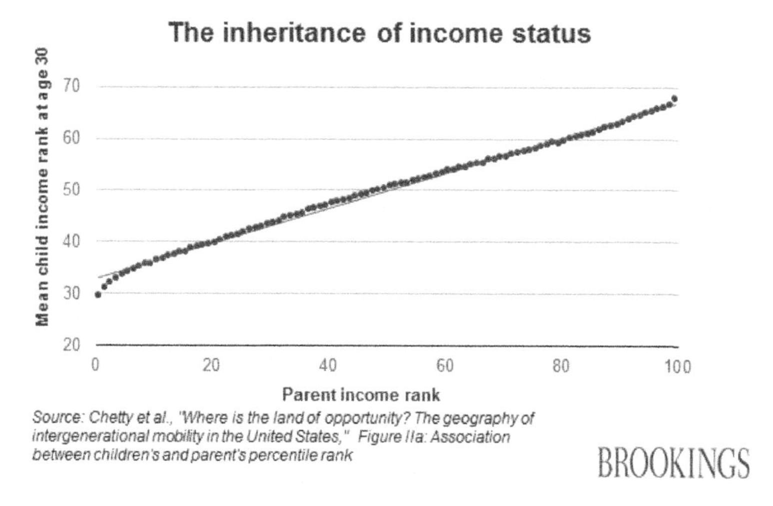

Figure 20. Correlation between income of parents and children

likelihood of making that economic leap is far greater in Canada and Denmark than in the US.

Figure 20 shows the direct correlation between a child's income and that of their parents. The data creates an almost perfectly straight line—a very high correlation. The higher the income of the parent, the higher the child's income will be at age thirty.

Given these two facts: 1) income and wealth are distributed in an extremely skewed manner, and 2) to a large extent people are locked into their station in life from birth—is there a moral imperative to change one or both situations? There are no absolutes when it comes to arguments of this nature. How one analyzes this problem, if it is deemed a problem, and how one might suggest making necessary changes depends upon one's philosophy of life. At one end of the spectrum might be those who would say the economy is a time-tested machine that distributes rewards in an efficient manner (an idea debunked earlier), and where one starts out in life is luck of the draw, it always has been and always will be that way. This would be the assessment of one to whom the market has been kind; a person one might say who was born on third base and has a short run to home plate. Away from that hardened position are gradations of views on how severe the problem is and how drastic the measures to remedy it should be. While one can only hope that most people are not unmoved when confronted with true hardship and suffering by other people, raw statistics are not the most-effective way to convey true hardship and suffering. Numbers such as 16 percent of the children in the US live below the poverty line (Poverty USA, 2019), 25 percent of all Americans deal with hunger on a regular basis, 20 percent of Americans live in unsafe housing, 20 percent of American children do not complete high school, 40 percent of students are unable to afford post-secondary education, infant mortality rates are three times higher for women in poverty than those in higher income brackets . . . these numbers do not do justice to the problem.

Most of us need to confront these harsh realities face-to-face to appreciate them. We need to visit a homeless shelter, serve food in a soup kitchen, sit in a classroom in an inner city school for a day, stand on a street corner with day laborers waiting for someone to drive by and give them one day of work. The fact of huge well-being disparities is not just a statistic in the economic literature. It is a set of numbers, each one with a face and a story—millions of them.

All modern religions have much to say about egregious inequality. But it is not necessary to go into books like the Bible or Torah or delve deeply into the moral teachings of any major religion to get a reflection point on what is going on in the US economy. Aside from the economic and social aspects of the huge inequality developing in the US, does it seem right that so many have so little, while so few have so much? Does it seem fair that some people worry about how to make a house payment or buy food for the month while others worry about which continent to visit on their next vacation? Is it equitable that some people are trapped by their housing situation into sending their children to schools where poor educational outcomes are a secondary worry to the physical safety of their children, while others pick and choose among elite private college preparatory schools?

Remember what philosopher John Rawls had to say on these issues. Rawls' views on fairness and justice were elegantly simple and intuitive. Again, in Rawls' paradigm we all start from an initial position. We are born randomly into a family that may be wealthy or dirt poor. We may be given a great mind and intellect, or we may end up with a mental handicap. Our body may be rugged, healthy, and athletic, or we may start with physical defects at birth that will set the tone for the rest of our lives. Rawls further says that our initial position is constructed behind a "veil of ignorance"; we do not know what circumstances will be dealt to us. Given equal odds of being born into abject poverty surrounded by people struggling to get through life or being born into a highly privileged station in life, how would we write the rules for this giant Monopoly game called the market?

By definition, our chances of being born in the top 10 percent of the economic ladder are only one out of ten—long odds. It is fair to say that all but the most reckless gamblers would opt for rules that tended toward leveling the playing field rather than rules producing skewed outcomes like those we see in the US now. If we don't know where we will be placed on the income distribution curve, and if the likelihood of moving very far from our starting point is limited, would we not choose a paradigm that tends toward more equality from the lowest to the highest points on the curve?

This black box we call the economic system produces many things, not the least of which is a population spread very unevenly with income and wealth. There are those among us living in conditions of extreme want while not far away are others living in unimaginable wealth. It strains credulity to think that this is either healthy or sustainable long term. As we have seen, wealth disproportionately loaded at the top end results in the economic engine continuing to work overtime to satisfy the wants of the wealthy while naturally tending to ignore the needs of the low-wage earners. This then sows discontent throughout the US society and drives wedges between segments of the US population. History tells us that this set of conditions never lasts forever.

Without wise, reasonable measures being taken to address these problems, history again tells us how resolution is found. If everyone's self-interest at all socioeconomic levels does not motivate us to aggressively undertake change, hopefully enough people have some inner voice that will continue to whisper, *This is not right*, until change is undertaken. The wide and growing gaps in well-being among the population is an existential threat to the order of the US society.

CHAPTER 8

SUGGESTED CHANGES

We Built it; We Can Rebuild it

Having discussed some of the inputs and outputs of the complex system we call the US economic system, or the market, we now set out some changes that flow from that discussion. Several questions and directions of further inquiry will also be introduced that will hopefully prompt further areas of study by economists, policymakers, and business leaders. To set the stage for what will follow, I will step briefly through the flow of inquiry in this book.

In the Introduction, the emphasis of the argument was that the US market is a complicated and interconnected system composed of economic, legal, and social components. Over the last 250 years in the US, we have woven those components into a tapestry that controls all US economic interactions, a constantly changing tapestry. Americans find themselves in 2021 in a place that is the result of the development of a system that did not evolve organically. No economic equivalent of evolution took the US here; Americans purposefully built this economic system.

Examining the ways Americans might take stock of the US system, we asked the question: Is the current system producing outputs, results, that Americans want to see? Given that the purpose of any economics system is to distribute, in one way or another, the scarce resources that are available, how do we evaluate whether the distributions made are fair and/or equitable? A methodology proposed for making those calculations was set out by John Rawls. His paradigm suggests how to build a system if one had the chance to start anew and rewrite the rules of the game: if no one knew in what time, location, or economic circumstance they would be born into, Americans might have a vastly different perspective on how they would, or would have, shaped the US economic system. For example, if the US system favors the top 1 percent of income earners, and the chance of being in that group is only one out of 100, rational people would write (or rewrite) the rules to be kinder to the other 99 percent.

We looked into the concept of private real property as it is written into US law and understood by generations of Americans. The vastly different timelines of the land and the people who temporarily occupy it were discussed in both economic and philosophical terms. A structure of stewardship versus ownership was set forth as one way to harmonize the inordinately different lifetimes of the land and the people.

Basic economics teaches that the US system is supposed to balance supply and demand throughout the economy. Looking more carefully at the concept of demand, we asked how demand registered in the current system. The more money or credit one has, the more one's demands are attended to by the market. The extent to which one's voice is heard in the market (the extent to which one's demands are registered) depends upon the resources one brings to the game. Peoples' demands vary across the economic spectrum and, given scarce resources, whose demands are met is a critical issue that is dependent upon many policy considerations.

Information and the part that it plays in the US economy was noted as a critical piece of the US market economy because, theoretically, consumers take information in, evaluate it, and make decisions on how to spend their money based on that information (the "rational man" paradigm now debunked). Information is a necessary ingredient in demand; the flow of information leads in large part to the creation of demand.

We explored externalities—the textbook example of market failures—those areas where costs are not borne by those receiving the benefits of a transaction, and situations where benefits flow to someone who does not pay the costs incurred in creating the benefit. Externalities abound in the US economy. Several large problems facing society, such as climate change and low wages, can be analyzed in the context of externalities.

We considered gross domestic product (GDP), the metric used to measure how much the US economy is producing, and the problems with what GDP is measuring and where the focus is directed in moving the US economy. The primary idea with the discussion of GDP is that efforts are focused on the things people measure. If people are missing important measures of societal well-being with a GDP calculation, they will not focus on improving what they are not counting.

Finally we discussed the implications for the US economy and US society resulting from the terrible imbalance in wealth and income. The economic, social, and moral implications of this imbalance in well-being were set out. The future health and tranquility of the US society are tied to the Gini coefficient.

The US economy comes up short in meeting the five basic economic determinants of human well-being set out in the Introduction. The system comes up short in providing *affordable housing* to everyone across the income spectrum. The quality of the US *food supply* is in question when so many people are "food insecure," and obesity and diabetes are at epidemic levels. The US *educational system* provides an excellent product to some, particularly those with higher incomes, and to many it is woefully inadequate, particularly for minorities and low-income people. High-quality *medical care*, not medical insurance, is not universally available to everyone in the US. And too many workers do not have *jobs that pay a living wage*. So how do we begin to move forward with meaningful change to the system?

Develop an accounting system that more accurately reflects human progress, not GDP

There is nothing quantitative in life that can be changed in a positive way until it can be measured in its current state; then one can begin to evaluate how it is performing. This leads back to GDP, the timeworn universally applied metric of how the US economy is performing. We started by positing that the economy is not delivering some fundamental things to all people that it should, it does not take account of the inter-temporal issues confronting one generation to the next, it is overusing the natural resources and increasingly allowing a very unequal allocation of resources among people. Hence, the economy is not working very well, or at least not optimally.

The first step on the road to remediation of the US economy must be revamping how we measure what this complex web of laws, rules, institutions, etc. does. More importantly, how do we prescribe an accurate measurement of what we want the economy to do? We need to move away from measuring activity to measuring outcomes. The US annual economic output totals approximately twenty trillion dollars as measured by current methods. That makes the US GDP about 30 percent larger than that of the nearest competitor, China. Back to the question raised earlier; does that matter? It matters only to the extent that it is measuring constructive activity. If it is measuring things that are despoiling US natural and human resources, a larger number is not a good thing. If increments in that GDP calculation arise from repairing damage

Americans have intentionally inflicted on US natural resources or infrastructure, incarcerating large numbers of people, extracting natural resources while degrading our air and water, and increasing labor output at wage levels that are sapping the health and overall well-being of the labor force, then GDP is sending false signals to US public policymakers and private sector decision-makers.

The United States and the rest of the world is undeniably wedded to the GDP calculation. GDP is not going to fade from the economic landscape anytime soon. A companion system of measuring the quality and quantity of US economic output needs to be constructed that operates parallel to GDP calculations. A fair amount of work has been done already to construct indices that measure meaningful economic output as opposed to less-valuable measures of economic activity—again, the difference between running 10 mph on a treadmill and going nowhere versus running 10 mph and actually moving 10 miles.

Paradigm shifts like this take years to burrow into academia, literature, and daily economic vernacular. As parallel methods of measuring economic output are developed, they should be used as a check on the time-worn GDP figures. If we see the US economy growing as measured by GDP but evolving and more refined indices are signaling that Americans are going backward, alarm bells should go off. If the measure of GDP says the economy is growing at a robust 3–4 percent per year, but life expectancies are not growing or may even be declining. If infant mortality rates are not declining, if incidences of chronic diseases like diabetes and heart disease are growing, if high school graduation rates are falling, if the percentage of people gaining post-secondary education is not rising, if the achievement gap between Whites and people of color fails to shrink, if the number of people who can afford healthcare and decent housing is not rising, if more US lakes and rivers are not becoming swimmable, and if Americans are continuing to eradicate species of animals, plants, and insects and the US weather is getting more and more volatile as the atmosphere continues to warm . . . then GDP is sending false signals. Americans are not becoming better off. GDP is going one direction and quality of life is going in the opposite direction.

Improving the metrics of the US economy should be one of the first and most important tasks for economists. Noteworthy in this effort are any steps being taken by countries to better evaluate the true health of their economies. New Zealand has just instituted a "well-being" budgeting process designed to evaluate national spending based upon whether or not it adds to national well-being. Bhutan has measured well-being for years with its economic indicators. Americans have the resources within US economics departments and business schools throughout the US university system to develop better metrics for the US economy.

It will probably be required that GDP be run side by side with a developing system that attempts to more accurately measure economic well-being. To illustrate: in 1948, the US GDP was $275 billion in nominal terms. By 2018 the economy had grown to $20 trillion, an increase of seventy times its size in the seventy years between 1948 and 2018. As measured by GDP, the economy grew tremendously in the last half of the twentieth century and the early years of the twenty-first century. But are Americans that much better off than in 1948? Are Americans any better off now?

A look into the GDP numbers is revealing and raises questions that constantly need to be asked. The percent of GDP spent on education grew from 0.3 percent of GDP in 1948 to about 1 percent in 2020. That 1 percent slice of economic activity that went to education held steady for over twenty years. The amount of GDP devoted to the financial services industry (banking, insurance, securities trading) grew from 2 percent of GDP in1948 to over 7 percent in 2020.[9]

Query: are Americans moving ahead by keeping a tight rein on the resources devoted to education while watching a growing part

9. US Bureau of Economic Analysis, 2020.

of the US national income going to banking, finance, and securities trading? Are Americans spending enough on education as the US global ranking of educational achievement continues to drop? The US continues to need programmers, engineers, and scientists from overseas to meet US domestic needs. The technical requirements of jobs in the economy grow steadily yet a relatively small number of primary and secondary students in the US have access to high quality STEM programs (science, technology, engineering, and math)? (ACT STEM, 2017)

Who is gaining as the US devotes more talent and resources to expanding US financial markets? The variety and complexity of financial instruments continues to grow. The markets for derivative-based financial products have exploded since 1990. More people and talent continue to go into the securities industry. As more complex financial instruments are created, household debt has grown, almost doubling between 2003 and 2019 (Catanzaro, 2020). The events of 2006 and 2007 revealed the soft underbelly of the burgeoning financial world. "Quants" (mathematics experts) working at the direction of a relatively small number of financial market executives, developed complex ways to make middle class people think they could afford larger and more-expensive homes. The ensuing housing bubble almost brought the entire financial world to its knees. Americans need to continually monitor the components of the US GDP (until there is something better to gauge the economy) looking for those parts of GDP that are growing and those that are shrinking. Do the parts of the economy experiencing growth contribute to the common good or individuals' well-being? Or are they incentivizing people to take huge risks for personal gain at the expense of the common good?

Every component that makes up the US GDP warrants scrutiny. In 1980, the addition to GDP from incarcerating prisoners in the US was about $17 billion. By 2017 that increment to GDP had grown to over $80 billion (Equal Justice Initiative, 2017). And that is merely the "operating" costs of having so many people in US prisons; that number does not include the capital costs of building hundreds of new prison facilities. Should incarcerating people be a profit center? What is the inevitable result from tying profitability to the number of prisoners behind bars?

Address pressing structural needs in the US, raise taxes

The overall tax liability in the US is too small. For comparative purposes, in 2018 US total tax revenues, both federal and state, were 24 percent of GDP. By comparison, in 2018 Canada's tax revenue was almost 33 percent of GDP, Britain's was 33 percent, Germany's was almost 37 percent. The average tax burden for OECD countries in 2018 was 34 percent of GDP (OECD, 2020). If total combined tax revenue, both federal and state, was increased by 5 percent of GDP, it would put the United States closer in line with other developed countries; tax revenue would increase by almost $1 trillion per year. That is a large amount of money by any definition. What would the country do with all this new revenue? Why raise taxes this much?

For a variety of reasons, increasing governmental revenue makes sense; but three reasons stand out. First, total governmental deficits have run over $700 billion for a number of years. Deficits increased to over $1 trillion annually during the Great Recession when US government spending increased to bail out failing financial institutions and stimulate the economy. In 2013 the deficit again dropped down to $679 billion and decreased for several years. That drop in the deficit ended in 2018 with the passage of a new tax bill that largely cut corporate taxes along with minor cuts to individual taxes. In 2019 the deficit exceeded $1 trillion and is projected to exceed that amount in outlying years. An increase in tax revenues could alleviate the constant deficit spending and possibly even begin to reduce the outstanding government debt, if that is even a goal worth chasing in the context of Modern Monetary Theory. This would, of course, completely reverse what was done in 2018 under the more recent tax legislation. Nonetheless, that outcome should be music to the ears of those who feel that the most important problem facing the US is the growing public debt. There are only two ways to reduce the deficit and pay off debt: spend less or take in more revenue. Spending less gets more difficult every year as larger percentages of federal spending are in the areas of Social Security, Medicare, Medicaid, defense, and interest on the debt.

The next two reasons to increase governmental revenue both deal with two unmet needs in the US. Much of the political rhetoric in recent years has centered on healthcare, specifically health insurance in the US. Ever since the passage of the Affordable Care Act (ACA) in 2010, factions in the US worked to repeal it and steps were taken to do just that. The conversation and rhetoric around repealing the ACA grew louder with the deepening partisan divides in Congress and across the nation. Many of the twenty million people who gained health insurance under the ACA did so through the portal of Medicaid, the program that funds health insurance for low-income and elderly or disabled people (Tolbert, et al., 2020). Subsidization of healthcare in the US runs at about $700 billion per year with the largest part of that going to support Medicaid and Children's Health Insurance Program (CHIP). The ACA itself is costing more than $50 billion/year. Repeal of the ACA would cause many millions of those who acquired insurance through Medicaid to lose it just as quickly. Total federal subsidies to healthcare totaled over $730 billion in 2019 according to the Congressional budget Office (CBO, 2019). The largest amount of that again going to Medicaid and CHIP. Healthcare is extremely expensive and until progress is made in the US on tackling the continually rising healthcare costs, providing health insurance to everyone in the country will require more money, not less.

The second seemingly universally agreed-upon need for more

money is in the area of infrastructure. People of almost all political persuasions seem to agree that the infrastructure in the US needs serious maintenance and upgrades. Almost every facet of the publicly owned fixed assets in the country need work. There are huge amounts of deferred maintenance in road and bridge repair and huge needs in water and sewer line repair (think Flint, Michigan). Many rural areas still need to be connected to municipal water systems where they can get access to non-polluted safe drinking water. Wind farms are being constructed in the West, South, and Midwest in locations into which power lines had not been built. Many school buildings in the US need significant upgrading. Providing adequate internet access to rural areas will require large investments much like was needed for the rural electrification project decades ago. In addition, the US is on the cusp of new higher-speed internet connectivity that will require substantial investments in equipment and hardware. The benefits of large infrastructure projects come in two ways: 1) improved infrastructure greases the wheels of the economy overall and makes the economy more efficient and productive, and 2) projects like this can create hundreds of thousands of jobs both during the construction phase and in the ongoing maintenance phase, all highly skilled and well-paying jobs that are immune to outsourcing.

In 2015 the Dutch consulting firm, Arcadis, undertook to estimate the total amount of infrastructure on the ground in most countries. The data, which came from World Bank and other sources, revealed some interesting comparisons. While to compile accurate figures for this data is difficult, the Arcadis study derived some good information. According to their data, China, as of 2015, led the word with total infrastructure in place at $48 trillion (US$). The United States comes in second at $37 trillion of infrastructure (Cayet & Cavalla, 2015). These levels of infrastructure combine both public and private assets. Other data in the study pointed to the low accretion to infrastructure in the US resulting in net disinvestment in infrastructure overall. The gap between infrastructure spending in the US and infrastructure needs continues to grow (Woetzel, et al., 2016).

Fixed assets deteriorate over time in private industry as they do in the public sector. This depreciation is recorded as depreciation expense on private company income statements. Private enterprises realize that they must account for the fact that their assets are depreciating over time, and they must record an expense reflecting this depreciation. Depreciation, a cost of doing business, reflects the fact that fixed assets are being consumed in the process of producing whatever it is a company produces. That depreciation expense reflects just how much must be spent to replace those assets and keep the level of fixed assets constant.

The same applies to public sector assets; they depreciate. Roads crumble, bridges rust and collapse, pipelines rot in the ground, buildings slowly deteriorate. All fixed assets have a useful life which varies by type of asset. If allowance is not made for replacing those assets over their life, when they are fully depreciated, they are gone. For example, in the power industry, once a coal-fired power plant is fully depreciated (i.e. has been depleted over its useful life), the output from that plant is gone forever unless the utility has been putting money back into the plant to replace that deterioration over time. The utility will no longer have electricity to sell to its customers unless the plant was continually refurbished or provisions for a replacement plant were made.

The same holds true of public sector infrastructure. Since 2000, public entities have been required to account for depreciation in their fixed assets similar to the accounting required in the private sector (Sage, 2014). Assets must be continually rebuilt or in time they are no longer serviceable. Roads can no longer carry traffic; pipelines can no longer carry water, oil, or gas; buildings can no longer safely accommodate students needing an education.

Every asset has a different useful life. Some assets may function for thirty years, others for fifty years, some longer. But no asset lasts forever. Assuming the Arcadis study is in the ballpark of an estimate of the infrastructure currently in place in the US at $37 trillion, the question is: what is the useful life of those assets? Even with the disparity in types of infrastructure and serviceable life of those assets, on average those assets likely do not have useful life of more than fifty years. Thus taking a conservative view, 2 percent of the total infrastructure should always be in the process of being rebuilt (1/50 of the asset base). That would require an outlay of $740 billion annually just to maintain the current infrastructure in the US which speaks to the fact that adequate resources are not being devoted to repair and replacement of fixed assets, not to mention the additions to the asset base necessitated by changing technology and general population growth. This level of expenditure makes the $750 billion public works program undertaken during the Great Recession in 2007 and the more recent calls for a trillion-dollar public works program seem like small change efforts. That $750 billion is a conservative estimate of what is needed on an annual basis to merely maintain what is already on or in the ground. It does not address additional upgrades to infrastructure. With population growth new streets are needed, new airports must be built, new transit systems must be constructed, new water and sewer lines constructed. Technological change will require rewiring vast amounts of the country; powerlines bringing new wind and solar sources to parts of the country not now connected; cabling and wiring to connect businesses, schools, and homes to higher speed internet. International trade will grow, requiring ports to be added and expanded and rail line capacity to be expanded. One-time programs on the order of $750 billion to $1 trillion are insufficient to keep US fixed assets intact, let alone add new highways, ports, pipelines, airports, schools, parks, and so on.

The shortcomings noted above deal just with the physical capital of the country. The inattention to and depreciation of the human capital in the US poses the greater threat to the future well-being of the country. When the health, well-being, and educational level of the population stagnates or moves backward, the economy loses ground. The educational achievement of students in the US continues to drop compared to students in many other developed countries. Poverty levels remain stubbornly high in the US and food insecurity remains a serious problem for large segments of the population. When people have to focus entirely on basic life functions to survive . . . paying the rent, buying groceries, clothing their children, trying to figure out how to pay for doctor visits for themselves and their children, it is impossible to focus on improving one's future and develop forward-looking goals, let alone implement plans on how to get there.

The deterioration in the physical and human capital in the US results from a huge underinvestment in both. The level of resources devoted to the "upkeep" of the country is not a result of natural forces working throughout the economy. The level of investment in the public sector exists by choice. Every year, tax and spending bills are brought before the US Congress and individual state legislatures. Decisions to either invest or not invest in infrastructure are debated and lobbied around very heavily. The condition of the US fixed assets is not an accident but a choice. Different choices can be made. Serious and ongoing investments need to be made in the US physical and human resource base if Americans are going to upgrade the housing stock in the country, regain the lead in education compared to the rest of the world, and provide more stable, well-paying jobs to a larger percentage of the workforce.

Aggressively address income and wealth maldistribution

Refer to the income distribution curve in the US in Chapter 7. The curve needs to be flattened. The Gini coefficient of income for the United States needs to be lowered significantly and steps need to be taken to assure that income distribution becomes less skewed to the upper incomes. The reasons for this, discussed previously, are threefold: 1) the social fabric of the country becomes frayed with a grossly unequal distribution of income, the US politics becomes acidic and dysfunctional as the population becomes a nation of haves and have-nots, 2) the US economy will function more productively and at a higher level with better income distribution, and 3) allowing gross disparities in well-being for the population due to societal structures we have created is morally wrong. We cannot tacitly assign large swaths of the population in the US to a meager, hard scrabble existence amid a sea of great wealth and consider that to be acceptable.

If we are to make progress in the US on areas discussed at the outset: universal access to decent, affordable housing; elimination of food insecurity, and making higher-quality food available to everyone, giving all people access to quality healthcare; assuring that anyone working full time can provide for their families; then the way in which people are compensated for their labor must change dramatically.

If we look at the income distribution curve and consider how we go about flattening the curve, we can begin by thinking about different segments of the curve, the low end of the curve and the high end of the curve. Let us start at the low-income end of the curve. As has been said in various ways by many, if you want to end poverty, give people money. Given that at any point in time, the amount of income that a country generates is fixed. If income distribution is to be evened out, those currently at the low end of the curve need to earn more money and those at the very top need to earn less or have more taken away from them in the form of higher income and estate taxes. That is axiomatic. To many, the notion of income redistribution sounds socialistic, going contra to everything seemingly at the core of the US economic system. Yet as argued herein, the very economic system that has created this massive disparity in income distribution has been purposefully created over time. The gross inequities in income in the US did not result from a natural flow of organic economic forces. The complex system that has delivered the current results has been purposefully built over time; it will need to be purposefully changed. And as the response to the COVID pandemic has taught us, the system can be changed quickly and significantly when the will of those in control dictates it should be.

The first remedial step to be taken is to raise the minimum wage. The argument against raising the minimum wage is that it will cost low earners their jobs. Low-income jobs will be eliminated by an increase in the minimum wage. Generally, the weight of economic study in this area says otherwise. Certainly, a few low wage jobs will be eliminated but not in any wholesale fashion. Not only does a low minimum wage affect those earning at that scale, but it also affects those in other low-skilled jobs that are being paid near the minimum wage level, but not much above it. A low minimum wage tends to anchor the wage scale at the less skilled end, at a low level. If the minimum wage were increased from $7.25 per hour to $15.00 per hour, it would impact many other jobs paying in the $15–$25/hour range. The debate about the minimum wage should begin with a serious discussion about the value and dignity of all work. At $7.25/ hour an individual earns $14,500 per year. The federal poverty guideline for a single person is $12,000 per year. For a two-person household the federal poverty guideline is $16,200. Add two children to the household, and the poverty level rises to $24,600. Two people working minimum-wage jobs would earn just above that amount: $30,000 per year.

Another fallacy that has some acceptance in the minimum-wage debate is that most people earning that wage are young kids working part time while in school. That is not the case. Over half of the people earning the minimum wage are supporting themselves or a family on that wage. Many people employed in minimum-wage jobs work in the agriculture sector and the service sector. They pick the fruits and vegetables that fill US tables; they bring food in the restaurants; they clean US hotel rooms; they staff the drive-through windows at the fast food restaurants where many Americans eat daily. If there is any activity that Americans need or want to have done, but cannot or choose not to do for ourselves, why should that person not earn a living wage to do that work? Are Americans comfortable knowing the person picking the vegetables for their salad is not able to provide for their own family by doing so? Would Americans be willing to pay a little more for lettuce if it meant someone toiling in the sun all day could feed their family on what they earned helping to feed American families? If Americans are not willing to pay people fairly to do things for us, then people should prepare to do more things for themselves. Everyone will need to grow very large gardens or stop by a community garden on the way home from work and pick their own dinner salad; restaurants should be no more than places to stop by and cook one's own food in the kitchen, clear one's own table, and wash one's own dishes before leaving; people should bring their own sheets to the hotel, make their own bed, strip it when they leave, and clean the bathroom on the way out. As for fast food . . . stop eating it, it wasn't good for people anyway. If Americans are willing to ask someone to do something for them, they should have the civility and sense of fairness to pay others enough to live on.

Americans need to change the focus of the discussion of wages at the low end of the scale from the minimum wage to a "livable wage." The two are vastly different. The nonpartisan think tank, Economic Policy Institute (EPI), has done a great deal of research on what it takes families of various sizes to live in all parts of the US. They have analyzed all components of a typical family's expenses and tailored them to individual parts of the country. They looked at housing costs, food, transportation, day care, medical costs, etc. By their calculations, the amount of money needed to "get by" in Des Moines, Iowa, in 2017 was $77,000 for a two-parent, two-child family. By contrast that same two parent two-child family needs $148,000 annually to get by in San Francisco. Contrast that with the 2017 federal poverty level of $24,600 for a family of four. That is a $52,000 difference between "poverty" and "getting by" in Des

Moines and a $124,000 gap between "poverty" and "getting by" in San Francisco. The amount of money it takes for a family to live varies dramatically from one part of the country to another; but clearly, no family can truly live anywhere if they are earning at the poverty level. The official poverty level which is still used to calculate eligibility for many assistance programs in the US, and is the basis around which much of our discussion of poverty centers, is based upon "three times the cost of a minimum food diet in 1963"(US Census, 2019). This number then gets adjusted for inflation. If there ever was a nonsensical approach to deriving such an important index, this is it. That would be akin to determining the average annual cost of a college education as something like five times the cost of textbooks for a college freshman. The entire notion of the poverty level needs to be rethought, and then scrapped. The economic bar should be raised for everyone to "getting by," not one or two times the poverty level. A more precise calculation of the cost for anyone to live should be built around the concept used by the EPI, not the antiquated calculation used by the Census Bureau.

So how might we structure a system that compensates people for the substandard wage they earn from their job? The US has a system like this in place now called the Earned Income Tax Credit (EIC). This credit was created in 1975 and adjusted and changed several times since then. The credit is a means of giving a cash credit to wage earners based upon the income of the recipient and the number or children they support. As with all parts of the Internal Revenue Code, detailed rules define each part of the credit: who is eligible, who is a qualifying child, the income levels at which it is phased out, etc.

Here is how the credit works under different scenarios. A single person does not qualify for the credit unless their adjusted income is less than $14,880 per year. Assuming that person is earning the federal minimum wage ($7.25/hour) they are earning approximately $14,500 per year and are on the edge of being eligible for the credit. If their earnings were somewhat lower, in the $13,000 per year range, they would qualify for a credit of $506. A married couple is not eligible for the credit if their combined income is greater than $20,430/year. If their combined income is below that threshold, they qualify for a $506 credit. Essentially people earning around the federal poverty level ($13,800 for a single person, and $18,600 for a two-person family) can earn $506 from the EIC. That just might buy frugal shoppers a month or so of groceries. That is hardly a game-changer for anyone's lifestyle.

Now look at a single person with a child to support. That person can earn up to $39,296 per year and still claim the tax credit. How much is the tax credit in that situation? $3,373. If a single person is supporting two children, s/he can earn up to $44,648 and earn a credit of $5,572. Two people earning the minimum wage (combined income about $29,000 per year) can earn that same additional $5,572, resulting in total household income, earnings plus EIC, of approximately $35,000 per year. If these two people's situation were such that they earned right at the EIC cutoff level ($50,198 for a married couple) and added the $5,572 EIC for two children, their household income would be $55,600. That is still about $22,000 below the $77,000 that the EPI estimated was required to "get by" in Des Moines, Iowa. Few would argue that a family of four is going to live very well on $55,000 per year or less, no matter where in the country they live.

The EIC makes a good vehicle for moving people up to a fair minimum level of earnings. The program takes tax revenue from higher up the income spectrum and distributes it back down the ladder to those trying to get by on low or relatively low wages. In that regard we already have an income redistribution system built into the US tax code. Conceptually nothing would change. What needs to change, however, are the parameters within which the program functions. In tax year 2019 over twenty-five million people and households earned a credit under the EIC provisions. The average credit received was $2,480. (EITC, 2020). That relatively small sum is not enough to make any significant change in the lifestyle of someone earning at the poverty level or some small multiple of the poverty level. For meaningful change to take place at the lower end of the income distribution curve, the benchmark upon which supplemental income is provided should not be the currently computed poverty level or something that is in close proximity to the existing minimum wage level. A tax credit designed to supplement income in order to get people to the "getting by" standard as set out by the EPI should be the target.

Giving an additional $500 to a single person earning at the poverty level or a married couple earning $20,000 is not a serious economic program, it is a ploy. Giving $5,000 to a couple raising two children on $30,000-$40,000 is cynical. The total income "redistributed" through EIC in 2019 was $63 billion. That is not a lot of money flowing from the top to the bottom. Consider, this is less than the wealth of one very wealthy American family, the Waltons who own Walmart. A much more robust program needs to be implemented to dramatically raise the bottom end of the income-distribution curve. It needs to be done for both economic and moral reasons. When people have greater income, they spend money, they buy things they need. If there is an impediment to economic growth today, it is lack of effective demand, not a lack of supply.

Demand in market economies is registered in dollars or other currencies. Without money or the access to credit, latent demand for any commodity or service goes unnoticed. Builders make houses for people that can afford to buy them, clothiers tailor clothes for those with cash to purchase their goods, GM builds cars for everybody that can buy their cars not for everyone who needs access to transportation.

The answers to some of the most perplexing US economic dilemmas are quite simple. For example, there is a shortage of housing for people with low incomes. Why? Precisely because low-income people do not have enough money to make the $1,500/month house payment needed to buy a $300,000 house, which is about the median home price in the country. Almost half of wage earners in the US earn less than $50,000 per year. A person needs to be earning over $50,000 per year to be able to afford to pay 30 percent of their income for housing and afford the median-priced home. That threshold eliminates over half of the people in the country. Where is the puzzle about why there is not enough low-income housing available? The unmet demands of low-income people need to be monetized by raising their wages.

People earning less than $35,000/year (over one-third of wage earners) cannot afford principal, interest, taxes, and insurance on a $125,000 house. There is not much housing in that price range being built. As income (demand) is concentrated in the very upper ends of the scale, higher-end housing will be built, more expensive cars will be produced, expensive vacation packages will be offered, and on and on. There is massive pent-up demand in the US and globally. It can only be addressed if the maldistribution of income is addressed. The benefits, both economic and social, that would flow from more equitable income distribution are dramatic. As John Kennedy said in his inaugural address in 1961, "This county cannot afford to be materially rich and spiritually poor."

Caps at the Top

If we are to get serious about a more just and justifiable income distribution, we will need to make significant adjustments to the top end of the economic scale and at the low end of the income scale. The top 1 percent of earners take home over 20 percent of all income. Cut that group in half, and the numbers are even worse: the top .5 percent of earners take home about 18 percent of national income. Wealth is even more maldistributed than income. The wealthiest 1 percent in the US have about 40 percent of all net worth, while the top .5 percent have 35 percent of the wealth. Whether the problem is stated in percentage terms such as this, graphically, or is described by the Gini coefficient, the reality is quite simple: a very few people earn most of the income and control most of the wealth, while vast swaths of the population struggle to survive, make ends meet, or as the EPI describes it, "get by."

If moving income from the top to the bottom is socialism, then moving income from the bottom and middle to the top was theft and fraud. This is precisely what has happened over the past forty years in the United States. Wealth and income have continually shifted in the US beginning in the 1700s and they have done so in response to laws, regulations, and customs written and created by those who have gained control over the process. Follow the money. Organic, no. Intentional, yes. The aristocracy in the South was created in the 1700s and 1800s on the premise that it was legal and moral to own people. The aristocracy in the early twentieth century was built on free or cheap land (the railroads), turning a blind eye to notions of competition upon which the US system was theoretically built (the oil and steel industries) and little tax liability to support the common good. Then in 1920 teetotalers grabbed the agenda and instituted Prohibition, which virtually eliminated the excise tax revenue, which in turn resulted in the federal government instituting an income tax. This began to put a lid on income gains for those at the top and gave lower-income people a chance to make up some ground on those at the top.

The two world wars forced the United States to more heavily tax people to support the wars. In addition to firmly entrenching the income tax in the US national fabric, the wars opened the US economy to the world through trade and hence began the road to globalization. Collective bargaining, which grew after World War II, was a tremendous benefit to the middle-class workers who were heavily unionized during this period. But unions have been under steady attack for at least thirty-five years. Tax rates have been lowered in the US, and large amounts of money have moved overseas in search of even lower tax rates. Entire industries have become wealthy by tapping into underpriced natural resources that belong to everyone, e.g. land, water, air, minerals, radio wave spectrums (coal, oil, gas, cattle grazing in the west, internet providers).

The ability to tax income and apply that revenue to any number of projects and processes is a powerful tool to move the US economy and the entire society in different directions. But Americans need to take even more robust steps to accomplish what needs to be achieved, a significant flattening of the income distribution curve.

In 1933 the Roosevelt administration attempted to institute a minimum-wage level for low-income workers in the US. The minimum wage was struck down by the Supreme Court in 1935, reinstituted in 1938, and finally given the legal blessing of the Supreme Court in 1941. Ironically, when it was first passed and in its nascent years, the minimum wage legislation was an attempt to bring wages up for workers in many low-income jobs. There was a tacit understanding that most wage earners, particularly in low-wage jobs, did not have the leverage to bargain effectively with their employers to get a livable wage. For several years before its passage however, the courts sided with employers and viewed setting a minimum wage as antithetical to a free-market economy.

The minimum wage has more effectively become a cap on the wages in many low-skilled and insufficiently valued jobs. States and municipalities have the legal option of raising the minimum wage in their jurisdiction above that mandated by federal legislation. This is being done or considered in many parts of the country. The most common wage level being bantered about is $15/hour versus the $7.25/hour level set by federal statute, though many states have minimum wage levels higher than the federal minimums. In real terms the federal minimum wage peaked in1968 and has been on the decline ever since. Inflation adjusted, the minimum wage in 1968 equated to $11.55 in 2019 dollars (Kurtz, et al., 2019). Minimum wage earners have lost a lot of ground since 1968. Bureau of Labor Statistics (BLS) data shows that in 1979 about 13 percent of wage earners were earning at or below the minimum wage level in effect at that time. By 2016 slightly fewer than 3 percent of wage earners were making less than or equal to the minimum wage level.

That percentage still equates to over two million wage earners being paid at or below minimum wage. Minimum wage earners work predominately in the food and service sectors of the economy. The low wages for these people need to be addressed, but raising the minimum wage for two million out of 136 million wage earners will not make significant progress on solving the income distribution gap.

In spite of the fact that the minimum wage is earned by only about 3 percent of wage earners, it does put a lid directly on what about two million people earn, and a tacit cap on what millions earning not too far above the minimum wage earn. Consider the impact if the income on the top two million income earners in the US was capped. That net would capture those earning in the top 1.5 percent in the US. Our reaction to the notion of capping low wages but not capping high wages is illogical and tears at our core beliefs about our economic system. If the US can legislate wage levels for low-income, less-skilled workers who are largely working in the private sector, why does the US moral indignation rise if Americans talk about capping wage levels for those in the highest of income levels? If we tell a private-sector company that an employee changing sheets in a hotel room or preparing food in a restaurant need only be paid $7.25 per hour, why should we not be able tell a hedge fund that it can only pay a trader $1 million per year, or that the CEO of the fund can only earn $10 million per year?

The reasons are simple and obvious. Those at the table writing the rules for the market are the wealthy and powerful, the high earners. Reflect on the John Rawls paradigm. If we did not know if we would end up being a $7.25 per hour service worker or a ten-million-dollar-a-year hedge fund executive, how would we write the rules? Before any of us picked up our first paycheck, the odds were that we would end up closer to the former group than we would end up in the latter group.

Setting wages levels at the low end of the curve seems very natural since the US has been doing that for over eighty years, dictating high-end wage levels feels very foreign to American's concept of how the US markets work. Why? The loudest argument for holding down the minimum wage level is that increasing that wage level will result in many low-income workers losing their jobs. Empirical studies on this question are not conclusive but generally do not support that conclusion. Let us apply similar logic at the high-income end of the spectrum. What would be the implications if the US capped hedge fund CEO pay at $10 million per year? Keep in mind this would be a tenfold or more reduction for many of the people in those positions. Would there soon be a shortage of people willing to take on the arduous task of managing a hedge fund if s/he could only earn $10 million? This question has never been put to a rigorous economic study, nor will it be. We know the answer to the question without rigorous empirical study. There are armies of bright market quants who would willingly take that modest pay level to run a hedge fund.

Would the quality of the hedge fund managers experience a dramatic drop if their pay were cut by 90 percent? Of course not. Legions of smart people could fill their shoes. So the argument is that with respect to low-wage jobs, we need to keep a tight lid on wage levels; because if we raise the wage from $7.25/hour to $15.00/hour, the market will eliminate the jobs (unlikely in a country that eats more meals at the drive-through window than the kitchen table). If we pay low-income workers more their jobs will go away; in contrast, unless we continue to pay high-end earners more and more, we will no longer get competent people to take those jobs. The US keeps low-wage earners employed by holding their pay down and keeps high-end earners employed by paying them ever more money.

Apparently supply and demand is alive and well at the low end of the ladder, but it ceases to function at multimillion-dollar pay levels. What is the economic theory behind unbridled and rapidly increasing income levels at the top of the pyramid? Is there a shortage of financial people willing to work for less than $100 million per year? Are attorneys billing $1,000/hour smarter and more skilled than those billing $200 to $500 per hour? If athletes could not make $20 million to catch a football or dribble a basketball, would kids all over the country stop playing ball and college athletes go back to the classroom? Were it not for the multimillion-dollar paychecks of heart surgeons, transplant surgeons, and other specialties, would we face a doctor shortage? No, of course not, we have a doctor shortage now; there are thousands turned away from medical school each year because of the limited seats available. Incomes at the top 0.1 percent and 0.01 percent continue to rise because people in those income brackets want them to, there is no economic rationale for such income levels, and there is no mechanism in place to keep a lid on the continuing upward spiral of income at those levels.

Americans need to undertake serious discussion about how compensation levels are set, controlled, and allowed to exist across the spectrum. This is not unbridled socialism; it is nothing more than injecting some basic rationality into the discussion of compensation. To state the issue in starker terms, we are extremely comfortable letting high-earning people set wage levels for low-earning people. Why should we not let low-income earners set the pay caps for high-income individuals? Compensation levels is another of those facets of the US system that Americans do not feel the necessity to think about too deeply or often because, "the market takes care of it, the market sets compensation levels." Who is the market? What is the process that sets compensation levels? An area crying out for more inquiry.

Low wages, another externality in the system

A classical economic analysis of low-wage earners would be as follows. A person earning $7.25/hour or a couple earning less than $50,000 per year and raising two children is likely getting a variety of forms of public assistance. They are very likely getting food stamps, receiving some type of assistance with healthcare such as Medicaid or at least a similar type of assistance for healthcare for their children, and possibly some type of heating or utility assistance to pay utilities during winter months. For illustrative purposes, we will assume that this individual is a single person working in the fast-food service and is supporting him/herself on the minimum wage $7.25/hour and earning $14,500 per year. The individual is not highly educated and has little other job experience and thus is consigned for now to the fast-food or similar industry. The employer can replace this worker quite readily as there are many similar unskilled workers who will take that job, many now coming from legal and illegal immigrant populations. Earning $7.25/hour, this individual cannot "get by." S/he requires some form of public assistance to survive. Who fills the gaps in their income? The general public, the taxpayers. Quite simply, this is an externality, which we discussed in a previous chapter. Let's go through an analysis showing how a low-wage worker is just another externality in the US system: There are many costs associated with selling hamburgers to people through the drive-up window. The business owner must make a lease payment or make a mortgage payment, buy the food ingredients that go into the sandwiches, pay his utilities, and pay the employees. Consider the reaction if the employer told a lessor that s/he could not pay $2,000/month for the lease and the lessor would have to get part of that money each month from the city or state. Consider if the employer told Sysco Corporation that s/he could only pay $3/lb. for ground beef and Sysco would need to get the remaining $2/lb. from the federal government. What if the employer told the gas company that s/he could only pay 80 percent of his utility bill; the utility would need to get in line with the low wage earner and pick up some utility assistance payments. This is of course absurd, yet this is exactly what happens to the wage component of the employer's cost structure. The employer cannot pay the employee the cost of the employee surviving, so the employee must go elsewhere to make up the difference.

The employee's cost is passed on to others who may not be going through the drive-through window . . . hence a classic externality, a disconnect between the total costs of providing a good or service and the person who receives the benefits, the business owner, or the customer.

The underpaid employee is an externality created by the employer, just as much as polluted air is an externality created by coal-fired utilities. The minimum cost of labor anywhere is the amount of money it takes for an employee to live, to get by, which varies significantly from place to place in the US. The cost of labor in San Francisco is double the cost of labor in Des Moines. If an employer cannot afford to pay that wage scale in San Francisco, s/he needs to move the operation.

Labor is just one of many inputs in most businesses. But if a business cannot pay labor enough to live on, it needs to rework the business model. It may need to pay the management team less. If electricity is a large cost, it may need to move to Washington State, which has lower utility costs than many states. If real estate is a factor, it may need to move to Omaha or Topeka. If these types of changes still do not allow the business to pay for its labor, it may just have to raise its prices. And if no one buys its products, then the business model is broken, and probably always was.

On a macro scale, the huge maldistribution of income juxtaposed against a backdrop of huge welfare programs points to the massive externalities that exist in the labor market in the US economy. Understanding and thinking about the income distribution problem as a problem of economic externalities may provide some clarity to policymakers as they look for ways to address the problem. It provides a framework within which to analyze the problem and devise solutions. If we arrive at a point where there is some consensus that anyone willing to work full time at a job, any job, should be able to support themselves and their family on the fruits of their labor, then the problem takes on a different look. There is no moral justification to ask someone to do something for us and not be willing to pay them a living wage to perform that task. If Americans are not willing to pay the person who shingles our house or landscapes the yard enough money to buy health insurance, people should strap on a tool belt and do it themselves. If Americans cannot pay the person serving the fast food lunch enough to heat their home in the winter, people should carry a lunch bucket to work. If Americans do not pay teachers enough to live in the communities where they teach and send their children to the schools where they teach, Americans should home school their children.

The glaring inequities in the US labor markets which cause the huge maldistribution problem has no single, simple solution, but the genesis of the problem is the same thing that bedevils other parts of the US economy discussed previously. The US has created what exists in the labor markets. It is not organic, and it can be changed if the will to do so exists.

The income distribution curve needs to become much less concave. The extent to which the curve needs to be flattened for economic and social reasons is an area ripe for study in a multi-disciplinary manner. Economists, psychologists, sociologists, ethicists, and others need to collaborate on assessing more optimal income distributions.

To efficiently address the maldistribution of income in the US economy, the prices of the labor inputs in US production processes must go up.

With an eye to Figure 21, which is a reminder of the income situation that needs to be addressed, the starting point for remediation of this issue is the bottom 50 percent of income earners. Over the past fifty years, the incomes of people in the 50th percentile of income and below have moved very little in real terms, while the incomes of those in the top 5 percent and 10 percent (95th and 90th percentiles) have risen significantly in real terms. Income of the bottom half of income earners can be addressed in one of three ways. The first way to deal with low income is to continue on the

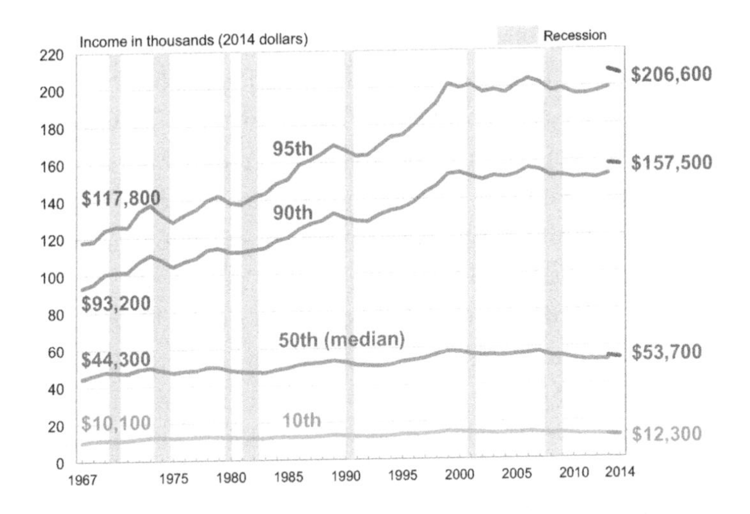

Note: The 2013 data reflect the implementation of the redesigned income questions. See Appendix D of the P60 report, "Income and Poverty in the United States: 2014," for more information. Income rounded to nearest $100.
Source: U.S. Census Bureau, Current Population Survey, 1968 to 2015 Annual Social and Economic Supplements.

Figure 21. Real household income at selected percentiles: 1967 to 2014

same path that's been followed for decades; allow low-income people to continue to struggle to make ends meet and attempt to make up their shortfalls with specific transfer payment programs such as food, medical, heating assistance, etc.

As Figure 21 shows, this has not, and will not, move the income line in any significant manner for the bottom half of the population. This allows the labor externality to continue to exist. The second way to transfer income to low-income earners is to tax income at the top of the scale, and transfer that income to the lower end of the scale. This could be done in the form of a significant increase in the marginal tax rates for very high earners or the imposition of a wealth tax, an idea discussed of late in some political circles in the US and which was argued for very cogently by Thomas Piketty in his book, *Capital in the Twenty-First Century* (Belknap Press, 2017).

Either or both of these tax approaches could be undertaken but would face huge ideological roadblocks. A mechanism would have to be developed to transfer the money taken in from the tax and distribute it on down the ladder. This might be accomplished through a mechanism like the Earned Income Tax Credit. This would be a simple transfer of income . . . a redistribution of wealth. That notion has many negative implications in the US political dialogue. The third option is to raise the wages of low-income earners in a real and meaningful way.

If the third option were followed, in theory how would that work? First, the bottom wage scales would be adjusted in line with the concept of getting by, as set out by the EPI, and raising it substantially above the currently discussed ideas about the minimum wage. The floor for wages would need to be adjusted upward to $20–$25/hour or more, depending upon the location in the country. In extremely high cost of living parts of the country such as San Francisco or New York, the "floor wage" would need to be set much higher than in lower-cost regions in the Midwest and South. Moving the floor wage higher would, of course, have the effect of pushing the entire bandwidth of wages that rest upon the current minimum wage, higher. For example, if a minimum wage service worker makes $12/hour and in the same community a delivery truck driver makes $18/hour, by moving the service worker's floor wage up to $20/hour, the delivery driver must now be paid on the order of $25/hour to keep him driving.

Substantially raising the floor wage will naturally raise the entire scale of wages above it. A broad-based increase in wages across the board would have several highly beneficial effects but if, and only if, the entire wage increase did not get translated into equivalent, across-the-board price increases. If wages went up 10 percent and the prices of everything went up 10 percent to absorb the wage increase, all that would have been accomplished is an increase in inflation across the board, and in relative terms no one's situation would have changed.

A significant wage increase, particularly for the bottom half of wage earners, would have several benefits if it were not completely offset by price increases. First, with low-income workers earning a living wage, the need for the massive transfer payments, required under the overly complicated and contrived federal assistance programs, would be significantly reduced. This would be the simplest way to improve the lot of millions of Americans. Rather than ending poverty by "giving people money" as the old saying goes, this is a way to end poverty by "letting people earn more money."

The concept of paying people a living wage, an amount sufficient to get by in the locale they find themselves, dovetails easily into the broader set of questions about the nature of work that needs to take place in the US. If Americans want the benefits of someone's labor, isn't it only right that they be paid enough to support themselves and their family with that work? If Americans are not willing to pay a person sufficiently then who are we asking to subsidize the benefits we receive from their labor but are not fully paying for? Who and what mechanisms have been at play that have resulted in the highly skewed compensation levels seen in the US? Why is it philosophically acceptable to legislate wages at the low end of the spectrum, but it tugs at all the US notions about free enterprise and capitalism to discuss touching the top end of the pay scale?

A second and very important benefit to raising wages (and here the importance of not offsetting wage increases by parallel price increases comes into focus) is that it will begin to reverse a trend that has been taking place for decades in the US, the ever-increasing share of the national income that goes to capital rather than labor. As Figure 22 depicts, labor's share of the national income pie has been declining in fits and starts since 1947 (FRED, 2020). Since about 2000, the decline in labor's share of income has been very pronounced, dipping from 64 to 58 percent of income by one calculation. There has been a great deal of study done to see the root causes of this trend.

Clearly the maldistribution of income in the US will only worsen if the trends in Figure 22 continue to play out. Piketty, in

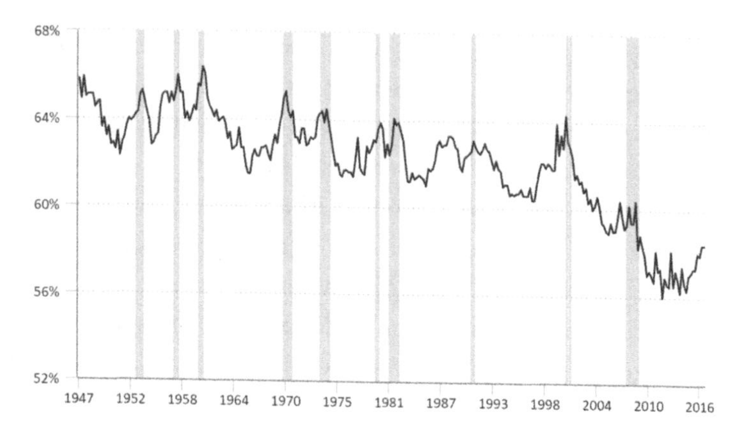

Figure 22. Labor's share of output in the nonfarm business sector

---

the conclusion of his book *Capital in the Twenty-First Century*, points out an underlying problem with capitalism that relates to this issue. As Piketty sets it out formulaically, when the return on capital is greater than the growth rate of the economy (r>g) for a period of time, capital will accumulate and the share of income going to capital will increasingly outstrip the share of income going to labor. That these conditions hold now, and have over long periods of history, is clear. With the economy in the US growing in the 3 percent range (probably unsustainable in the long run) and the labor force increasing, all that 3 percent growth will not accrue to labor; a small percentage of it will.

The returns on capital can be viewed in different ways. Using the return on the S&P 500 stock index as a proxy, the return on capital might be pegged around 7 percent over the last decade, though it can vary widely over time. As the return on capital remains high, capital will accumulate, and more of the national income pie will accrue to capital not labor. There is a benefit, if not a necessity, to keeping a lid on the return on equity across the board. In order to chip away at the wealth distribution problem, wages need to go up and stay in the pockets of wage earners. If wage increases are all pushed back onto the consumer, then prices go up, profit margins remain the same, returns to shareholders remain intact, and nothing has changed with respect to capital v. labor. The cost of living has gone up, low-wage earners are no better off, and wealth continues to accumulate at the same rate at the higher-income levels.

This does not suggest that a simple fix to this problem exists. Returns vary by industry and by company. One thing is eminently clear: large tax cuts to corporations only exacerbate the problem by swiftly increasing the after-tax returns to their shareholders (capital). Wealth needs to be taxed in one form or another to slow the massive and disproportionate accumulation of wealth in so few hands. It can be taxed at the individual level or the level of its creation, the corporate level. There is no justification (economic, societal, or moral) for large profitable corporations to pay little or no income taxes.

Companies that paid no federal taxes in 2018 include Amazon, Chevron, Halliburton, General Motors, IBM, and Eli Lily. Most of the taxes saved by these corporations did not go to their employees, i.e. labor, it went to shareholders, i.e. capital. As discussed previously, the long-term and growing economic divergence between the few and the many in the US is not sustainable.

Final Thoughts

The question this book asked from the outset was whether the system was delivering results that Americans are satisfied with. This basic question provided the perspective through which I examined several parts of the system. On many levels the system is falling short. The market is not meeting the basic needs of many people. The market is not giving everyone a chance to bring themselves up by their bootstraps. The market is not treating everyone fairly or equitably, by any definition.

America's capitalist free-market system is not producing what many Americans would like to see as the output of this complex machine. Health outcomes for much of the population are poor; the educational achievements of a large numbers of people fall short of what they should be, and gaps in racial achievement persist; access to decent and affordable housing is not widespread enough; natural resources continue to be degraded; the country is extremely deficient in being able to monitor and manage the national balance sheet; and differences in well-being between population cohorts continue to increase. If as a nation Americans are content with this, there is little left to be done. But if Americans want the economy to give us better results, it *can* happen. Remember, there is nothing organic about this economic system; people built it, people can change it. Measures taken almost overnight to address the COVID pandemic attest to the fact that significant changes can be made throughout the economy when there is a willingness to do so. Change must begin with a serious conversation about the value of work . . . all work. COVID-19 brought this conversation to the forefront. It gave us answers we need to think very hard about, and remember. During 2020, essential workers were identified as ICU nurses and doctors, teachers, police and firefighters, hospital cleaning staff, meat packing plant workers, grocery store employees, delivery truck drivers. Among those not considered "essential workers" were the managers of hedge funds, CEOs of large corporations, professional athletes, investment bankers, and other highly compensated people. The disconnect between how essential a job is and the compensation it receives should be the new starting point for discussion about the value of work.

Like everyone else, my experiences inform my views, the lens through which I see and understand them. I have spent a lot of time in the last eighteen years tutoring students in the Minneapolis and St. Paul schools. I am one of a large group of tutors who come from relatively well-off backgrounds to work with these students. These students put a face on the economic system of the United States.

Who are these students? They are low-income children,

almost all qualify for free or reduced lunch, most are minority: Hispanic, African American, Asian students. They come to school from areas of the city full of low-income housing. At times I have worked with students that the school bus picked up at homeless shelters. The parents of these students work, often in restaurants, hotels, nursing homes, service jobs, construction jobs, doing hard work. College or advanced education is not part of their life experience, and therefore not on the radar screen of their future. The lines separating the tutors and students are stark. To understand how the American system works and does not work, it is necessary to attach faces to it. Complex mathematical models are not always the best way to understand economics. If we do not see the system in terms of the people whose lives are formed and controlled by the market, complex models are not going to shed much enlightenment on our understanding of economics.

If Americans want more robust and reliable demand in the economy and a better track record of meeting everyone's basic needs, then the United States needs to significantly increase incomes of the lower 50 percent of the population and simultaneously, through one mechanism or another, halt the unabated income and wealth growth by the top 1 percent. If Americans are looking for producers to respond to consumers' desires and needs, we must be attentive to the information being provided to consumers, in particular the veracity of that information. If Americans are going to continue to rely on markets to fairly and efficiently allocate scarce resources, then business models must include all their true costs; externalities that continue to allow environmental degradation, and the spreading of labor costs across the community rather than charging the company's customers need to be eliminated. If America is going to produce better economic performance for the entire population, we need to start measuring the things that matter; stop relying on GDP as the numeraire that tells us how well we are doing.

Any of the problems that plague the US economy can be

solved. We created the system; we own it; we can change it. Americans can reimagine how the economic system can and should work to create a fairer and more equitable society for all, not a few, and for generations to come.

BIBLIOGRAPHY

Abbott. (October 26, 2016). New Study: Babies Fed Infant Formula With 2'-Fl Human Milk Oligosaccharide+ Had Immune Response More Like Breastfed Babies. Press Release. https://abbott.mediaroom.com/2016-10-26-New-Study-Babies-Fed-Infant-Formula-with-2-FL-Human-Milk-Oligosaccharide-Had-Immune-Response-More-Like-Breastfed-Babies.

ACT. American College Test. (2017). STEM Education in the US: Where We Are and What We Can Do|2017. https://www.act.org/content/dam/act/unsecured/documents/STEM/2017/STEM-Education-in-the-US-2017.pdf.

Adams, Maurianne, Lee Anne Bell, & Pat Griffin (Eds). (2007). History of Racism and Immigration Time Line, Racial Equity Tools: Key Events in the Struggle for Racial Equity in the United States. *Teaching for Diversity and Social Justice*, Second Ed., Routledge. https://www.racialequitytools.org/resourcefiles/racismimmigration-timeline.pdf.

American Cancer Society medical and editorial content team. (Sept 10, 2014). American Cancer Society Recumbinant Bovine Growth Hormone. https://www.cancer.org/cancer/cancer-causes/recombinant-bovine-growth-hormone.html https://www.cancer.org/content/dam/CRC/PDF/Public/622.00.pdf.

Arner, Douglas. (2002). Development of the American Law of Corporations to 1832. *SMU Law Review*. Rev. 23. Vol 55. Iss 1. https://scholar.smu.edu/smulr/vol55/iss1/6.

Associated Press. (September 17, 2011). Montana: Settlement Approved for Asbestos Victims. *The New York Times*. http://www.nytimes.com/2011/09/17/us/montana-settlement-approved-for-asbestos-victims.html.

Bargh, J.A. & J.S. Uleman (eds). (1989). Conditional automaticity: Varieties of automatic influence in social perception and cognition. In *Unintended thought*. Guilford Press, 51–69.

Barrionuevo, Alexei. (October 4, 2005). Egg Producers Relent on Industry Seal. *The New York Times*.

Baumeister, R., E. Masicampo, & K. Vohs. (2011). Do conscious thoughts cause behavior? *Annual Review of Psychology*. 62, 331–361. doi: 10.1146/annurev.psych.093008.131126.

Beasely Allen Law Firm. (November 27, 2007. Settlement Reached in Acid Rain Case. https://www.beasleyallen.com/news/settlement-reached-in-acid-rain-case/.

Berchick, Edward R., Jessica C. Barnett, & Rachel D. Upton. (November 2019). Current Population Reports, P60-267(RV), Health Insurance Coverage in the United States: 2018. Washington, DC: U.S. Government Printing Office. https://www.census.gov/content/dam/Census/library/publications/2019/demo/p60-267.pdf.

Berg, H., M. Söderlund, M., & A. Lindström. (2015), Spreading joy: examining the effects of smiling models on consumer joy and attitudes. *Journal of Consumer Marketing*. Vol. 32 No. 6, 459–469.

Blaug, Mark. (1996). *Economic Theory In Perspective.* UK: Cambridge University Press.

Bohner, G., & N. Dickel. (2011). Attitudes and attitude change. *Annual Review of Psychology*, 62, 391–417.

Bowman, Zach. (April 2, 2019). It's Not Just You: Cars are Crazy Expensive. *Road and Track*, https://www.roadandtrack.com/car-culture/buying-maintenance/a27016809/new-car-msrp-increase-2019/.

Carey, Nick. (March 1, 2018). GM, rivals chase luxury pickups' fat margins as US market dips. Reuters. https://www.reuters.com/article/us-gm-pickuptrucks/gm-rivals-chase-luxury-pickups-fat-margins-as-u-s-market-dips-idUSKCN1GD69K

Cartwright, Mark. (November 22, 2018). Feudalism. Ancient History Encyclopedia. https://www.ancient.eu/Feudalism/.

Catanzaro, Mark. (April 22, 2020). A Snapshot of Record-High US Household Debt. Federal Reserve Bank of St. Louis. https://www.stlouisfed.org/open-vault/2020/april/snapshot-record-high-household-debt.

Cayet, Julien, & Alasdair Cavalla. (2015). Global Built Asset Wealth Index 2015, Arcadis. https://www.arcadis.com/media/8/1/D/%7B81DC63EB-831F-41F3-BB8E-542031D8E3A6%7D9385_Global%20Built%20Asset%20Wealth%20Index%202015_FINAL%20WEB.pdf.

Center for Disease Control and Prevention. (September 28, 2020). Heart Disease Facts. https://www.cdc.gov/heartdisease/facts.htm?CDC_AA_refVal=https%3A%2F%2Fwww.cdc.gov%2Fdhdsp%2Fdata_statistics%2Ffact_sheets%2Ffs_heart_disease.htm.

Center for Poverty & Inequality. (September 2020). What is the Current Poverty Rate in the United States? University of California, Davis. https://poverty.ucdavis.edu/faq/what-current-poverty-rate-united-states.

Center on Budget and Policy Priorities. (2017). Policy Basics: Special Supplemental Nutrition Program for Women, Infants, and Children. Updated April 26, 2017. www.cbpp.org/research/food-assistance/policy-basics-special-supplemental-nutrition-program-for-women-infants-and#:~:text=How%20Is%20WIC%20Funded%3F,receives%20approximately%20%246%20billion%20annually.

Central Intelligence Agency. (n.d.). The World Factbook. Country Comparison: Distribution of Family Income. Gini Index. https://www.cia.gov/library/publications/the-world-factbook/fields/223rank.html.

Chetty, Raj, Nathaniel Hendren, Patrick Kline, Emmanuel Saez, & Nicholas Turner. (January 2014). Is the United States Still a Land of Opportunity? Recent trends in intergenerational mobility. National Bureau of Economic Research, Working

Paper 19844. Cambridge, MA. https://www.cia.gov/library/publications/the-world-factbook/fields/223rank.html.

Clemens, Austin. (December 9, 2019). Eight graphs that tell the story of US economic inequality. Washington Center for Equitable Growth, Washington, DC. https://equitablegrowth.org/eight-graphs-that-tell-the-story-of-u-s-economic-inequality/.

Congressional Budget Office. (May 2, 2019). Federal Subsidies for Health Insurance Coverage for People Under Age 65: 2019 to 2029. Report. https://www.cbo.gov/publication/55085#:~:text=CBO%20and%20JCT%20project%20that,and%20%241.3%20trillion%20in%202029.

Congressional Budget Office. (July 9, 2019). The Distribution of Household Income, 2016. Report. https://www.cbo.gov/publication/55413.

Cornell Law School. (n.d.). Legal Information Institute: Alienable. https://www.law.cornell.edu/wex/alienable.

DeSilver, Drew. (February 15, 2017). US students' academic achievement still lags that of their peers in many other countries. Pew Research Center, Washington, DC. HTTPS://WWW.PEWRESEARCH.ORG/FACT-TANK/2017/02/15/U-S-STUDENTS-INTERNATIONALLY-MATH-SCIENCE/.

Dowie, Mark. (September/October 1977). Pinto Madness *Mother Jones*. http://www.motherjones.com/politics/1977/09/pinto-madness.

Equal Justice Initiative. (February 6, 2017). Mass Incarceration Costs $182 Billion Every Year, Without Adding Much to Public Safety. Montgomery, Alabama: EJI. https://eji.org/news/mass-incarceration-costs-182-billion-annually/.

Eswaran, H., R. Lal, & P.F. Reich. (2001). *Land Degradation: An overview*. In: Bridges, E.M., I.D. Hannam, L.R. Oldeman, F.W.T. Pening de Vries, S.J. Scherr, & S. Sompatpanit (eds.).*Responses to Land Degradation*. Proc. 2nd. International Conference on Land Degradation and Desertification. Khon Kaen, Thailand. New Delhi: Oxford Press. https://www.nrcs.usda.gov/wps/portal/nrcs/detail/soils/use/?cid=nrcs142p2_054028.

Eurostat. (July 24, 2019). Statistics Explained. *Quality of life indicators*. https://ec.europa.eu/eurostat/statistics-explained/index.php/Quality_of_life_indicators.

Facebook Investor Relations. (April 29, 2020). Facebook Reports First Quarter 2020 Results. Press Release. https://investor.fb.com/investor-news/press-release-details/2020/Facebook-Reports-First-Quarter-2020-Results/default.aspx.

FAO Commission on Genetic Resources for Food and Agriculture. (2019). The State of the World's Biodiversity for Food and Agriculture. http://www.fao.org/state-of-biodiversity-for-food-agriculture/en/.

Fisher, Jonathan, David Johnson, Jonathan P. Latner, Timothy Smeeding, & Jeffrey Thompson. (April 19, 2018). Estimating the marginal propensity to consume using the distributions of income, consumption, and wealth. Washington Center for Equitable Growth Working paper series. https://equitablegrowth.org/working-papers/marginal-propensity-consume/.

Fisher, Jonathan, David Johnson, Timothy Smeeding, & Jeffrey Thompson. (April 19, 2019). Estimating the Marginal Propensity to Consume Using the Distributions of Income, Consumption and Wealth. Federal Reserve Bank of Boston Working Paper No. 19-4. https://papers.ssrn.com/sol3/papers.cfm?abstract_id=3374467.

Flowers, Barbara. (May 2018). The Economics of Natural Disasters. Federal Reserve Bank of St. Louis. https://research.stlouisfed.org/publications/page1-econ/2018/05/03/the-economics-of-natural-disasters#:~:text=Generally%2C%20a%20region's%20economic%20activity,negative%20effects%20on%20economic%20growth.&text=GDP%20may%20fall%20in%20the,a%20positive%20effect%20on%20GDP.

Flowers, Nancy (Ed). (1999). *Human Rights Here and Now: Celebrating the Universal Declaration of Human Rights.* Minneapolis: Human Rights Educators' Network, Amnesty International USA, & Human Rights Resource Center. http://hrlibrary.umn.edu/edumat/hreduseries/hereandnow/Part-5/7_udhr-full.htm.

FRED. (August 9, 2020). Monetary Base. Board of Governors of the Federal Reserve System (US). Total Federal Reserve Bank of St. Louis. https://fred.stlouisfed.org/series/BOGMBASE.

FRED. (November 17, 2020). Economic Data. Board of Governors of the Federal Reserve System (US), Capacity Utilization: Total Index (TCU). https://fred.stlouisfed.org/series/TCU.

FRED. (August 14, 2020). US Bureau of Economic Analysis. Value Added by Private Industries: Finance, Insurance, Real Estate, Rental, and Leasing: Finance and Insurance as a Percentage of GDP. Federal Reserve Bank of St. Louis. https://fred.stlouisfed.org/series/VAPGDPFI.

FRED. (November 9, 2020). US Bureau of Labor Statistics. Nonfarm Business Sector: Labor Share. Federal Reserve Bank of St. Louis. https://fred.stlouisfed.org/series/PRS85006173.

FRED. (July 10, 2020). US Census Bureau and US Department of Housing and Urban Development. Median Sales Price for New Houses Sold in the United States. Federal Reserve Bank of St. Louis. https://fred.stlouisfed.org/series/MSPNHSUS.

FRED. (2020). US Census Bureau. Homeownership Rate for the United States. Federal Reserve Bank of St. Louis. https://fred.stlouisfed.org/series/RHORUSQ156N.

GNH Centre Bhutan. (n.d.). GNH Happiness Index. http://www.gnhcentrebhutan.org/what-is-gnh/gnh-happiness-index/.

Goehring, Karen, C., Barbara J. Marriage, Jeffery S. Oliver, Julie A. Wilder, Edward G. Barrett, & Rachael H. Buck. (December 2016). Similar to Those Who Are Breastfed, Infants Fed a Formula Containing 2'-Fucosyllactose Have Lower Inflammatory Cytokines in a Randomized Controlled Trial, *The Journal of Nutrition*. Vol 146, Issue 12. 2559–2566. https://doi.org/10.3945/jn.116.236919.

Good, M., C. P. Sodhi, Y. Yamaguchi, H. Jia, P. Lu, W.B. Fulton, L,Y. Martin, T. Prindle, D.F. Nino, Q. Zhou, C. Ma, J.A. Ozolek, R.H. Buck, K.C. Goehring, & D.J. Hackam. (2016). The human milk oligosaccharide 2'-fucosyllactose attenuates the severity of experimental necrotising enterocolitis by enhancing mesenteric perfusion in the neonatal intestine. *The British Journal of Nutrition. 116*(7). 1175–1187. Online at Cambridge University Press. https://doi.org/10.1017/S0007114516002944.

Gramer, Robbie. (March 24, 2017). Infographic: How Does U.S. Health Care Stack Up to the Developed World? *Foreign Policy*. HTTPS://FOREIGNPOLICY.COM/

2017/03/24/INFOGRAPHIC-U-S-HEALTH-CARE-COMPARED-TO-THE -REST-OF-THE-WORLD-NOT-PRETTY-TRUMP-CARE-PAUL-RYAN -AFFORDABLE-HEALTHCARE-ACT/.

Grandview Research. (April 2018). US Tobacco Market Size, Share & Trends Analysis Report By Product Type (Cigarettes, Smoking Tobacco, Smokeless Tobacco, Cigars & Cigarillos). Competitive Landscape And Segment Forecasts, 2018–2025. https://www.grandviewresearch.com/industry-analysis/us-tobacco-market.

Granheim, Sabrina Ionata , Katrin Engelhardt, Patti Rundall, Stella Bialous, Alessandro Iellamo, & Barrie Margetts. (2017). Interference in public health policy: examples of how the baby food industry uses tobacco industry tactics. *World Nutrition.* www.babymilkaction.org/wp-content/uploads/2018/11/WN-Tobacco .pdf.

Haidt, Jonathan. (2006). *The Happiness Hypothesis: Finding Modern Truth in Ancient Wisdom.* New York: Basic Books.

Harris, Alexander. (March 7, 2020). US Self Storage Industry Statistics. Updated March 7, 2020. Sparefoot Storage Beat.www.sparefoot.com/self-storage/ news/1432-self-storage-industry-statistics/.

Hirsch, Jerry. (June 3, 2020). General Motors and Ford Can Juice Profits by Shedding Models. *Trucks.* https://www.trucks.com/2020/06/03/gm-ford-should-shed -models/.

Hobijn, Bart & Alexander Nessbacher. (June 29, 2015). The Stimulative Effect of Redistribution. *FRBSF Economic Letter*. Federal Reserve Bank of San Francisco. https://www.frbsf.org/economic-research/publications/economic-letter/2015/ june/income-redistribution-policy-economic-stimulus/.

Hostetter, Martha & Sarah Klein. (September 27, 2018). In Focus: Reducing Racial Disparities in Health Care by Confronting Racism. The Commonwealth Fund. https://www.commonwealthfund.org/publications/newsletter-article/2018/sep/ focus-reducing-racial-disparities-health-care-confronting.

Index Mundi. (Jan 1, 2020). Gini Index (World Bank Estimate). https://www.index mundi.com/facts/indicators/SI.POV.GINI/compare#country=cu:eg:ly:sy.

Institute for Health Metrics and Evaluation. (April 24, 2019). Global malaria spending $2 billion short of WHO target, stifling progress toward eliminating disease. www.healthdata.org/news-release/global-malaria-spending-2-billion-short -who-target-stifling-progress-toward-eliminating#:~:text=News-,Global%20 malaria%20spending%20%242%20billion%20short%20of%20WHO,stifling% 20progress%20toward%20eliminating%20disease&text=SEATTLE%20%E2% 80%93%20A%20first%2Dof%2D,by%20the%20World%20Health%20Organi zation.

Internal Revenue Service. (Jan 16, 2020). Statistics for Tax Returns with EITC. https://www.eitc.irs.gov/eitc-central/statistics-for-tax-returns-with-eitc/statistics -for-tax-returns-with-eitc.

Internal Revenue Service. (Feb 2020). Historical Highlights of the IRS. https://www .irs.gov/newsroom/historical-highlights-of-the-irs.

Internal Revenue Service. (Apr 16, 2020). SOI Tax Stats-Historical Table 23. https:// www.irs.gov/statistics/soi-tax-stats-historical-table-23.

Jiang, Y., & H. Koball. (2018). Basic Facts about Low-Income Children: Children under 18 Years, 2016. New York: National Center for Children in Poverty. Columbia University Mailman School of Public Health. http://www.nccp.org/publications/pub_1194.html.

Joint Center for Housing Studies of Harvard University. (2011). America's Rental Housing Meeting Challenges, Building on Opportunities. https://www.jchs.harvard.edu/sites/default/files/americasrentalhousing-2011.pdf.

Kangas, Olli. (December 2000). Distributive Justice and Social Policy: Some Reflections on Rawls and Income Distribution. Social Policy & Administration. *International Journal of Policy and Research*. https://onlinelibrary.wiley.com/doi/abs/10.1111/1467-9515.00208.

Keating, Martha. (June 2001). Cradle to Grave: The Environmental Impacts from Coal. Clean Air Task Force, Boston, MA. https://www.csu.edu/cerc/research reports/documents/CradletoGrave-TheEnvironmentalImpactsFromCoal2001.pdf.

Kurtz, Annalyn, Tal Yellin, & Will Houp. (April 9, 2019). The US minimum wage through the years, *CNN Business*. https://www.cnn.com/interactive/2019/business/us-minimum-wage-by-year/index.html.

LaHaye, Laura. (n.d.). Mercantilism, The Library of Economics and Liberty. https://www.econlib.org/library/Enc/Mercantilism.html.

Letter. To James Madison from Thomas Jefferson. (September 6, 1789). National Archives. Founders Online. https://founders.archives.gov/documents/Madison/01-12-02-0248.

Love Money. (August 27, 2020). The world's 101 biggest private landowners: Discover who really owns the planet. https://www.lovemoney.com/gallerylist/70168/the-worlds-101-biggest-private-landowners.

Makary, MD, Marty. (2019). *The Price We Pay: What Broke American Health Care—and How to Fix It*. UK: Bloomsbury Publishing.

Market Watch. (2020). Annual Financials for CoreCivic Inc. https://www.marketwatch.com/investing/stock/cxw/financials.

Milstone, Nancy Hughes. (1986). A Common Law Solution to the Acid Rain Problem. *Valparaiso University Law Review*. Vol. 20 No. 2,.277–297. Winter. https://scholar.valpo.edu/cgi/viewcontent.cgi?article=1531&context=vulr; the author argues for changes to the law requiring utilities to internalize their costs of polluting.

Muller, David. (December 3, 2018). As more cars disappear, affordability challenge grows. *Automotive News*. https://www.autonews.com/article/20181203/RETAIL01/181209966/as-more-cars-disappear-affordability-challenge-grows.

Murray, Peter Noel, Phd. (Feb 26, 2013). How Emotions Influence What We Buy, *Psychology Today*. www.psychologytoday.com/us/blog/inside-the-consumer-mind/201302/how-emotions-influence-what-we-buy.

Nafziger, Steven & Peter H. Lindert. (2012). Russian Inequality on the Eve of Revolution. NBER Working Papers 18383. National Bureau of Economic Research, Inc.

National Ocean Service. (n.d.). National Oceanic and Atmospheric Administration US Department of Commerce. A Brief History of Pollution. https://oceanservice.noaa.gov/education/tutorial_pollution/02history.html.

National Oceanic and Atmospheric Administration. (August 1, 2019). Large 'dead zone' measured in Gulf of Mexico: Hurricane Barry dampens initial size predictions. US Department of Congress. https://www.noaa.gov/media-release/large-dead-zone-measured-in-gulf-of-mexico.

New York City Bar. (February 2016). Advancing The Right To Housing In The United States: Using International Law as a Foundation. Report By The International Human Rights Committee Of The New York City Bar Association. https://www2.nycbar.org/pdf/report/uploads/20072632-AdvancingtheRighttoHousingIHR2122016final.pdf.

NIH. (1991). Bovine Somatotropin. Technology Assess Conf Statement; 1990 Dec 5-7. Bethesda (MD): National Institutes of Health, Office of Medical Applications of Research:(7):16. https://consensus.nih.gov/1990/1990BovineSomatotropinta007html.htm#:~:text=As%20currently%20used%20in%20the,as%20those%20from%20untreated%20cows.

OECD. (2019), Biodiversity: Finance and the Economic and Business Case for Action. Report prepared for the G7 Environment Ministers' Meeting, 5–6 May 2019. https://www.oecd.org/environment/resources/biodiversity/G7-report-Biodiversity-Finance-and-the-Economic-and-Business-Case-for-Action.pdf.

Oklahoma Geological Survey. (April 21,2015). Statement on Oklahoma Seismicity. http://wichita.ogs.ou.edu/documents/OGS_Statement-Earthquakes-4-21-15.pdf.

Organization for Economic Cooperation and Development. (2020). OECD Stat. International Transport Forum. https://stats.oecd.org/Index.aspx?DataSetCode=ITF_INV-MTN_DATA#.

Organization for Economic Cooperation and Development. (2020), Tax revenue (indicator). doi: 10.1787/d98b8cf5-en. https://data.oecd.org/tax/tax-revenue.htm.

Organization for Economic Development and Cooperation. (February 16, 2006). Glossary of Statistical Terms, Gini Index. https://stats.oecd.org/glossary/detail.asp?ID=4842.

Ortega, Ralph. (November 25, 2019). How a handful of families control the most land in the US—and the majority are old and white: Billionaires Jeff Bezos, Ted Turner, Stan Kroenke, and John Malone are among 50 private landholders who own a total of 31 million acres between them. Mail Online. https://www.dailymail.co.uk/news/article-7724605/Who-owns-land-America-50-private-land-owners-control-31-MILLION-acres.html.

Our World In Data. (2017). Food Expenditure. United States Department of Agriculture (USDA) Economic Research Service. https://www.ers.usda.gov/data-products/food-expenditures.aspx.

PD&R Edge. (September 2014). Rental Burdens: Rethinking Affordability Measures. https://www.huduser.gov/portal/pdredge/pdr_edge_featd_article_092214.html#:~:text=HUD%20defines%20cost%2Dburdened%20families,of%20one's%20income%20on%20rent.

Pope John Paul II. (1991). *Centesimus Annus*. Rome: Libreria Editrice Vaticana Encyclicals.

Pope John Paul II. (1981). *On Human Work: Laborem Exercens*. Charleston, SC: Pauline Books & Media.

Poverty USA. (2019).The Population of Poverty USA, Poverty Facts. United States Conference of Catholic Bishops. https://www.povertyusa.org/facts.

Race Forward. (April 13, 2006). Historical Timeline of Public Education in the US. The Center for Racial Justice Innovation (formerly the Applied Research Center). https://www.raceforward.org/research/reports/historical-timeline-public-education-us.

Rebell, Michael A. (December 12, 2018). Major Federal Right to Education Lawsuit Filed in the U.S. Oxford Human Rights Hub Blog. OxHRH. http://ohrh.law.ox.ac.uk/major-federal-right-to-education-lawsuit-filed-in-the-u-s.

Reich, Charles. (1995). *Opposing the System*. New York, NY: Crown Publishing Group.

Rinat, Zafrir. (December 9, 2013). Food for Thought: How Rich Countries Exploit the Resources of Poorer Ones—and Get Away With It. https://www.haaretz.com/rich-nations-still-exploiting-world-1.5333127.

Ritchie, Hannah. (June 20, 2017). What the history of London's air pollution can tell us about the future of today's growing megacities. *Our World in Data*. https://ourworldindata.org/london-air-pollution#:~:text=The%20dominant%20contributor%20to%20London's,such%20as%20railways%20and%20waterways).

SAGE. (2014). Government Accounting for Fixed Assets. Sage Fixed Assets. https://www.sage.com/na/~/media/site/Sage%20Fixed%20Assets/docs/GASB_Accounting.pdf.

Salviati, Chris. (October 9, 2019). 2019 Cost Burden Report: Half of Renter Households Struggle with Affordability. *Apartment List*. https://www.apartmentlist.com/rentonomics/cost-burden-2019/.

Samito, Christian. (2009). *Becoming American Under Fire*. Ithaca, NY: Cornell University Press.

Say, J.B. (1803). *A Treatise on Political Economy*. New York: Augustus M. Kelley.

Scott, Bruce R. (December 2006).The Political Economy of Capitalism. Harvard Business School Working Paper. No. 07-037. https://www.hbs.edu/faculty/Pages/item.aspx?num=23129.

Sigal, Samuel. (June 8, 2019). Forget GDP—New Zealand is prioritizing gross national well-being. *Vox*. https://www.vox.com/future-perfect/2019/6/8/18656710/new-zealand-wellbeing-budget-bhutan-happiness.

Snyder, Thomas, D. (Ed). (1993). US Department of Education, Office of Educational Research and Improvement. National Center for Education Statistics. 120 Years of American Education: A Statistical Portrait. https://nces.ed.gov/pubs93/93442.pdf.

Squatriglia, Chuck. (June 9, 2008). Rising Gas Prices Finally Kill The Once-Mighty SUV. *Wired*. https://www.wired.com/2008/06/rising-gas-pric/.

Stone, Chad, Danilo Trisi, Arloc Sherman, & Jennifer Beltrán. (January 13, 2020). A Guide to Statistics on Historical Trends in Income Inequality. Center on Budget and Policy Priorities. https://www.cbpp.org/research/poverty-and-inequality/a-guide-to-statistics-on-historical-trends-in-income-inequality.

Strathern, Paul. (2004). *A Brief History of Economic Genius*. New York: Texere Publishing.

Struzik, Ed. (June 14, 2010). As the Far North Melts, Calls Grow for Arctic Treaty, Yale Environment 360. https://e360.yale.edu/features/as_the_far_north_melts_calls_grow_for_arctic_treaty.

Sweet, Ryan. (August 13, 2017). How Natural Disasters Affect US GDP, Moody's Analytics. https://www.economy.com/economicview/analysis/296804/How-Natural-Disasters-Affect-US-GDP.

Teutsch, PhD, Rabbi David. (November15, 2016). Attitudes, Beliefs and Values Shaping Jewish Practice. Reconstructing Judaism. https://www.reconstructingjudaism.org/article/attitudes-beliefs-and-values-shaping-jewish-practice.

The Law Dictionary. (n.d.). What is Fee? Black's Law Dictionary. Online legal dictionary, 2nd Edition. https://thelawdictionary.org/fee/.

The National Law Center on Homelessness and Poverty. (June 2011). "Simply Unacceptable": Homelessness and the Human Right to Housing In the United States 2011. A report. Washington, DC: NLCHP. https://nlchp.org/wp-content/uploads/2018/10/Simply_Unacceptable.pdf.

The United Nations Human Development Report (2019). Life Expectancy for Countries. Infoplease. https://www.infoplease.com/world/health-and-social-statistics/life-expectancy-countries#bycountry.

The World Bank. (2020). Understanding Poverty. Poverty and Shared Prosperity 2020 in *Reversal of Fortune*. https://www.worldbank.org/en/understanding-poverty.

The World Bank. (2018). Life expectancy at birth, male (years). https://data.worldbank.org/indicator/SP.DYN.LE00.MA.IN?end=2018&most_recent_value_desc=true&start=2016&view=chart.

Tolbert, Jennifer, Kendal Orgera, & Anthony Damico. (November 6, 2020). Key Facts about the Uninsured Population, KFF. https://www.kff.org/uninsured/fact-sheet/key-facts-about-the-uninsured-population/.

Touryalai, Halah (July 2, 2012). "Shady Overdraft Fees Could Cost Banks Over $1 Billion." *Forbes*.

Tracy, Paul. (September 30, 2020). Net Cash Flow. InvestingAnswers. https://investinganswers.com/dictionary/n/net-cash-flow.

Union of Concerned Scientists (January 2007). Smoke, Mirrors & Hot Air: How ExxonMobil Uses Big Tobacco's Tactics to Manufacture Uncertainly on Climate Science. Cambridge, MA: UCS. https://www.ucsusa.org/sites/default/files/2019-09/exxon_report.pdf.

United Health Foundation. (2018). America's Health Rankings. Annual Report: International Comparison. https://www.americashealthrankings.org/learn/reports/2018-annual-report/findings-international-comparison.

United Nations. (2015). Department of Department of Economic and Social Affairs. Transforming our world: the 2030 Agenda for Sustainable Development. Sustainable Development Goals. https://sustainabledevelopment.un.org/post2015/transformingourworld.

United Nations Development Programme. (2020). Human Development Report 2020. Human Development Index (HDI) Ranking. http://hdr.undp.org/en/composite/HDI.

United Nations. Peace, dignity and equality on a healthy planet. Water. https://www.un.org/en/sections/issues-depth/water/.

United States Conference of Catholic Bishops. (2005). Seven Themes of Catholic Social Teaching. Washington DC: USCCB 5-315. Communications. http://www.usccb.org/beliefs-and-teachings/what-we-believe/catholic-social-teaching/seven-themes-of-catholic-social-teaching.cfm.

United States Environmental Protection Agency. (n.d.). Understanding Global Warming Potentials. Greenhouse Gas Emissions. https://www.epa.gov/ghgemissions/understanding-global-warming-potentials.

University of Virginia Library. (n.d.). Distribution of Slaves in United States History. US Census Bureau in Thomas' Legion. http://thomaslegioncherokee.tripod.com/distributionofslavesinunitedstateshistory.html.

US Census Bureau. (January 25, 2016). Gini Index. https://www.census.gov/topics/income-poverty/income-inequality/about/metrics/gini-index.html.

US Census Bureau. (December11, 2019). The History of the Official Poverty Measure. https://www.census.gov/topics/income-poverty/poverty/about/history-of-the-poverty-measure.html#:~:text=The%20current%20official%20poverty%20measure,account%20for%20other%20family%20expenses.

US Census Bureau. (July 9, 2020). Real Median Household Income in the United States. Federal Reserve Bank of St. Louis. https://fred.stlouisfed.org/series/MEHOINUSA672N.

US Department of Agriculture. (2020). National School Lunch Program. Economic Research Service. www.ers.usda.gov/topics/food-nutrition-assistance/child-nutrition-programs/national-school-lunch-program/#:~:text=In%20fiscal%20year%20(FY)%202019,total%20cost%20of%20%2414.1%20billion.

US Department of Labor.(n.d.). History of Federal Minimum Wage Rates Under the Fair Labor Standards Act, 1938–2009. https://www.dol.gov/agencies/whd/minimum-wage/history/chart.

US Energy Information Administration. (June 17, 2020). How much carbon dioxide is produced when different fuels are burned. https://www.eia.gov/tools/faqs/faq.php?id=73&t=11.

US Energy Information Administration. (November 2, 2020). What is US electricity generation by energy source? https://www.eia.gov/tools/faqs/faq.php?id=427&t=3.

US FDA. (April 23, 2020). Report on the Food and Drug Administration's Review of the Safety of Recombinant Bovine Somatotropin. US Food and Drug Administration. http://www.fda.gov/AnimalVeterinary/SafetyHealth/ProductSafetyInformation/ucm130321.htm.

USDA Economic Research Service. (December 2019). Current Population Survey Food Security Supplement. https://www.ers.usda.gov/topics/food-nutrition-assistance/food-security-in-the-us/key-statistics-graphics.aspx.

Van den Bergh, Jeroen. (2008). The GDP Paradox. *Journal of Economic Psychology*. https://dnr.maryland.gov/mdgpi/Documents/GDP_Paradox.pdf.

Van Zee, Art, MD. (February 2009). The Promotion and Marketing of OxyContin: Commercial Triumph, Public Health Tragedy. *American Journal of Public Health*. 99(2) 221–227. https://www.ncbi.nlm.nih.gov/pmc/articles/PMC2622774/.

Ventola, C. Lee. (October 2011). Direct-to-Consumer Pharmaceutical Advertising, Therapeutic or Toxic? Pharmacy and Therapeutics. NIH. https://www.ncbi.nlm.nih.gov/pmc/articles/PMC3278148/.

Ventura, Luca. (November 26, 2018). Wealth Distribution and Income Inequality by Country 2018. *Global Finance*. https://www.gfmag.com/global-data/economic-data/wealth-distribution-income-inequality.

Warner, Ethan, Daniel Steinberg, Elke Hodson, & Garvin Heath. (August 2015). Potential Cost-Effective Opportunities for Methane Emission Abatement, Joint Institute for Strategic Energy Analysis. Technical Report. NREL/TP-6A50-62818. https://www.nrel.gov/docs/fy16osti/62818.pdf.

Weissmann, Jordan. (March 5, 2013). How Wall Street Devoured Corporate America, *The Atlantic*. https://www.theatlantic.com/business/archive/2013/03/how-wall-street-devoured-corporate-america/273732/.

Winberg, Steven. (June 26, 2020). Clean Coal is Crucial for American Jobs, Energy Security, and National Supply Chains. US Department of Energy. https://www.energy.gov/articles/clean-coal-crucial-american-jobs-energy-security-and-national-supply-chains.

Winter, Michael. (2012). Cigarette firms must run ads saying they lied. *USA Today*. http://www.usatoday.com/story/news/nation/2012/11/27/judge-orders-tobacco-ads-declaring-deception/1730211/.

Woetzel, Jonathan, Nicklas Garemo, Jan Mischke, Martin Hjerpe, & Robert Palter. (June 14, 2016). Bridging Global Infrastructure Gaps. McKinsey Global Institute. https://www.mckinsey.com/industries/capital-projects-and-infrastructure/our-insights/bridging-global-infrastructure-gaps#.

Wong, Alia. (November 28, 2018). The Students Suing for a Constitutional Right to Education. *The Atlantic*. https://www.theatlantic.com/education/archive/2018/11/lawsuit-constitutional-right-education/576901/.

World Economic Forum. (January 24, 2019). A New Circular Vision for Electronics, Time for a Global Reboot. https://www.weforum.org/reports/a-new-circular-vision-for-electronics-time-for-a-global-reboot.

World Economic Outlook Database. (October 2020). International Monetary Fund. https://www.imf.org/external/datamapper/datasets/WEO.

World Hunger Education Service (September 2018). Hunger in America: United States Hunger and Poverty Facts. https://www.worldhunger.org/hunger-in-america-united-states-hunger-poverty-facts-2018/.

World Population Review. (2020). Incarceration Rates by Country 2020. https://worldpopulationreview.com/country-rankings/incarceration-rates-by-country.

Yglesias, Matthew. (May 10, 2016). 25 hedge fund managers earned more last year than every kindergarten teacher in America. *Vox*. https://www.vox.com/2016/5/10/11648746/hedge-fund-manager-earnings.

ACKNOWLEDGMENTS

At times I wish I had written this book sooner, but had I done so, it would have been a vastly different book. It took time for ideas and thinking to mature and develop. The seeds for this book were planted in classrooms at the University of Iowa many years ago. My academic understanding of the economy was then tested and compared against years of work in the business world, the judicial system, and in the trenches working with dozens, if not hundreds, of low-income students in the parochial school system of Minneapolis and St. Paul. I want to sincerely thank a handful of people who critiqued every word of this book as it went along. Special thanks go to my brother, John, who had a long career in the banking industry and a penchant for detail; my lifelong friend, Jan Boresi, who has one of the sharpest accounting minds in the field and continually raised challenging questions; and my son, Nick, who is both a student of economics and psychology without whose encouragement this project may never have come to fruition. Thanks also to my wife, Deborah, who put up with countless hours of time being taken up at the computer and countless hours of my rambling on obscure parts of the economy. My deepest appreciation.

ABOUT THE AUTHOR

Richard McGuire has BS and MA degrees in economics from the University of Iowa. He received his JD from Mitchell Hamline School of Law. His career began in the railroad industry in the investment area for the Soo Line Railroad Company while in law school. He spent ten years in the banking industry in investments and balance sheet management for Bankers Trust Company in Des Moines, Iowa; TCF Bank in Minneapolis; and First Minnesota Savings Bank. He took his experience in the banking and the railroad industries into private law practice representing banks and short line railroads. He has litigated cases in Minnesota State Courts, US Bankruptcy Court, and before the Minnesota Supreme Court. McGuire spent the past twenty years in the rail car leasing business, during which time he started a rail car leasing company for a group of private investors and began his own business of buying, selling, and leasing rail equipment.

Over that same twenty-year period that McGuire worked in rail car leasing, he founded and managed a nonprofit tutoring group, the Catholic Tutor Corps. This group has placed volunteer tutors in over a dozen Twin Cities inner-city Catholic grade schools. His professional experience, combined with his time working with low-income, and minority students, watching the struggles they face, informed much of his thinking for this book.